—— 国际警务英语系列 ——

INTERNATIONAL POLICING

国际警务

INTERNATIONAL POLICING

★★★主　编　苏　竞★★★

重庆大学出版社

内容提要

本教程对国际警务方面的热点及重点问题进行了梳理和选编。教材内容涉及国际社会对这些问题的前沿探讨，主要的议题涉及：跨国有组织犯罪、国际经济犯罪、毒品走私、恐怖主义、国际刑警组织、维和等。教材共分为10个单元，每单元包含两篇英文文章，并配备背景知识、单词注解及案例分析。

图书在版编目(CIP)数据

国际警务／苏竞主编．—重庆：重庆大学出版社，2015.1

(国际警务英语系列)

ISBN 978-7-5624-8792-0

Ⅰ.①国…　Ⅱ.①苏…　Ⅲ.①公安—英语—教材　Ⅳ.①H31

中国版本图书馆CIP数据核字(2014)第306592号

国际警务

主　编　苏　竞

责任编辑：杨　琪　李　懿　　版式设计：杨　琪

责任校对：谢　芳　　责任印制：赵　晟

*

重庆大学出版社出版发行

出版人：邓晓益

社址：重庆市沙坪坝区大学城西路21号

邮编：401331

电话：(023) 88617190　88617185(中小学)

传真：(023) 88617186　88617166

网址：http://www.cqup.com.cn

邮箱：fxk@cqup.com.cn (营销中心)

全国新华书店经销

重庆五环印务有限公司印刷

*

开本：720×960　1/16　印张：13.75　字数：211千

2015年1月第1版　2015年1月第1次印刷

ISBN 978-7-5624-8792-0　定价：29.50元

前　言

随着全球一体化进程的加速，犯罪活动也呈现出国际化有组织性的特征。这种新的形势对世界各国的执法机构带来了全新的挑战——各国警方必须要加大力度推进国际警务合作，携手共同打击跨国犯罪和国际犯罪。在这样一个大背景下，我国部分公安院校开设了涉外警务以及英语（国际警务方向）专业，旨在培养出一批熟悉国内外国际执法的相关法律法规，掌握国际警务知识以及与之相关的专业执法技能的高素质警务人才。

为了适应培养这类人才的需要，湖北警官学院国际警务系根据实际教学需要，精心编写了国际警务系列教材。这本《国际警务》是其中的分册之一。本书将对国际警务方面的热点及重点问题进行梳理和选编。教材内容涉及国际警务的前沿问题。主要的议题涉及：跨国有组织犯罪、国际经济犯罪、毒品走私、恐怖主义、网络犯罪、人口贩卖与走私、国际警务合作、国际刑警组织、维和等。教材共分为 10 个单元，每单元包含两篇英文文章。每单元还包括背景知识、单词注解、练习以及案例分析。

本书由苏竞主编。在整个教材编写的过程中，编者参照了大量的国内外书籍及文献资料，引用了国内外相关调研报告、案例汇编和业务资料，以及相关图片与图表。在此，一并向上述书籍、文献资料、图片（表）的原作者表示衷心的感谢。

由于编写时间仓促，编者水平有限，疏漏之处在所难免，敬请各位同行、读者批评指正。

编　者

2014 年 9 月

Contents

Unit 1

International Organized Crime

Part I In-class Reading

Pre-reading Questions

- *Before reading the text, please discuss your personal thoughts on the definition of transnational organized crimes with your classmates.*
- *After reading the passage, do you agree on the definition of TOC given by the author? Why?*
- *Have you ever known TOC before? Could you name some crimes conducted by transnational organized criminal groups?*

Text A

Defining and Measuring Transnational Organized Crimes

Transnational criminal activity has increased in scale and extent, becoming a complex worldwide threat. Transnational criminals ignore borders. They move sums of money through the international financial system that are so huge they dwarf the combined economies of many nations. They are often organized in multi-crime businesses, and they have capitalized on growth in international communications and transportation to expand their criminal operations and form potent alliances. The corrosive activities of transnational criminal groups in the post-Cold War era no longer threaten particular countries or regions. They threaten all nations. Transnational organized crime is not only a law enforcement problem, but also a formidable and increasing threat to national and international security.

Transnational organized crime is not something completely new, but there is no standard, universally accepted definition of these kinds of criminality in the criminological and criminal law theories. The problem of definition is an important factor contributing to the inability of international law enforcement bodies to identify the size and scope of transnational organized crime accurately. Efforts to form a definition were made many times, but they only made this problem more difficult or created new problems.

We must admit, that a variety of other definitions, with all their diversity, nevertheless include the following essential elements and features, which are typical for transnational organized crime communities.

First, the activity of such organizations is criminal by nature, breaks legal taboos and must carry a penalty within existing procedures of law enforcement organs. It is obvious that a majority of social systems consider the so-called informal (hidden) economic activity, which is the bulk of organized transnational criminality, to be illegal and destructive to the development of the formal, legal economy. It breaks business laws and overturns normal economic activity. And this "essence" is a necessary element of the definition of transnational organized crime.

Second, despite the banality of this statement, it is very important to fix the fact that subjects in this activity is expediently executed, by people, who are intentionally united into a group (but more often cooperating groups) under the guidance of their established leaders. Hereby, the fact that they are well organized is not ephemeral and temporary. It is a key, constituent element of the phenomenon and definition of transnational organized crime.

Third, an essential constituent feature of transnational organized crime is the most important goal of the full spectrum of its activities. Any activity must be gainful. Bank fraud, blackmail, prostitution, theft of automobiles, drugs and weapons trafficking are equally acceptable if it makes a profit.

The fourth essential element of the transnational criminal rings is in the particular way they achieve their main goal, namely, in their readiness to use violence and bribery for the accomplishment and protection of their interests. Violence and bribery very often accompany each other, and are used deliberately with premeditation, in particular circumstances and to solve quite specific problems.

Thus, transnational organized crime rings act outside the law with the goal to make a profit and use bribery and violence for the realization and defense of group interests. These characteristics do not add anything special into the description of the phenomenon that has existed many years ago. At the same time, there are some distinctions inherent in it today, which increase to a new level the danger to the global social peace and stability. In particular, the ability to carry out global operations differentiates transnational criminal rings and organizations from traditional organized crime groups. The last one is rooted in the national territory of specific states, and even if they develop foreign connections in some cases, they do not operate on the wide international level. They act on the territories, regions or cities mostly within the national jurisdiction of a single state. For example, the American Mafia, which is also called La Cosa Nostra, is a very well known example of such a criminal syndicate. La Cosa Nostra appeared in the 1930s as a result of a conflict among Sicilian immigrant gangs in American cities. Despite the fact that its members introduced their ethnic traditions into the new community, La Cosa Nostra has never been a dummy organization or instrument of the Sicilian Mafia. It is really an American criminal organization. Although La Cosa Nostra was not without transnational connections, mainly they were for the purchase of alcohol and heroin from foreign illegal structures.

New transnational criminal groups are essentially different from national, domestic organizations more than anything else by the fact, that they were either created or transformed especially for criminal activity at a high level and international standard. The Colombian cartels are the most typical for such organizations. They correspond to vertically integrated global business, which has hundreds of thousands of employed specialists and associated workers in service. The Chinese Triads equally belong to the transnational generation of criminal groups, though they do not have such a strict structure. But their foreign operations are very intensive, very often in the flow of increasing Chinese immigration.

Transnational organized crime possesses a powerful potential and is highly dynamical. Therefore, it possesses a serious danger to the existence of both single states and the world community as a whole. Transnational criminal groups are very well organized and equipped. It is extremely difficult for law enforcement organs to find their way into the organizational structures of these groups, because many of them are based on ethnicity and act in the spheres of jurisdiction of different states. Transnational criminal groups use violence and bribery. Their activity undermines the authority of legal power and weakens democratic institutions. They destroy financial markets and economies of many states. The governmental resources that are designed to solve many social and economic problems are not enough to offset the criminal organizations at all. Many of them consolidate their connections with militant, ethnic, and religious movements.

A series of factors boosts the potential of transnational criminal rings. They act as parasites, for example, in cases where there are weak governments which have neither the resources nor political power to oppose them. They prosper on the fantastic amounts of money which they get as a result of illegal activity, particularly the production and sale of drugs. They are able to benefit from the increasing migration of people through countries and continents. Modern sophisticated weapons and appropriate technologies, which they have at their disposal, are effective means for the realization and protection of interests of transnational criminal groups. The inability of many states and international organizations to design and coordinate effective anti-criminal programs creates a favorable climate for the criminal community to maneuver in their resistance to law enforcement organs. So it is extremely important to develop the appropriate countermeasures to transnational organized criminal activity.

The main kinds of transnational organized crime activity consist of the following illicit businesses: illegal migration, trafficking in women and children, trafficking in body parts, corruption, theft and illegal export of cultural property, theft and trafficking in automobiles, fauna and flora trafficking, computer crimes, software piracy, nuclear material theft and trafficking, trafficking in firearms, trafficking in drugs, money laundering. No doubt, there can be identified other organized crime activities which have a transnational character or transnational implications. But in any case, if there is some uncertainty about the categorization of particular organized criminal activities in the mentioned range, however, their most common and distinctive feature is that it involves the crossing of borders or national jurisdictions. Therefore, control measures are especially important on the international level and also within affected countries if these measures have international implications.

(1, 251 words)

Background Information

▶ American Mafia

The American Mafia, commonly known as the Mafia, Italian Mafia, Italian Mob, or the Mob in the United States, is an Italian-American criminal society and offshoot of the Sicilian Mafia. Its members usually refer to it as Cosa Nostra. It emerged on the East Coast of the United States during the late 19th century following waves of Sicilian and Southern Italian emigration. There are five main New York City Mafia families, known as the Five Families: the Gambino, Lucchese, Genovese, Bonanno and Colombo families. At its peak, the Mafia dominated organized crime in the U.S. While each crime family operates independently, nationwide coordination is provided by the Commission, which consists of the bosses of each of the strongest families. Law enforcement still considers the Mafia the largest organized crime group in the United States. It has maintained control over much of the organized crime activity in the United States and certain parts of Canada.

The structure of American Mafia:

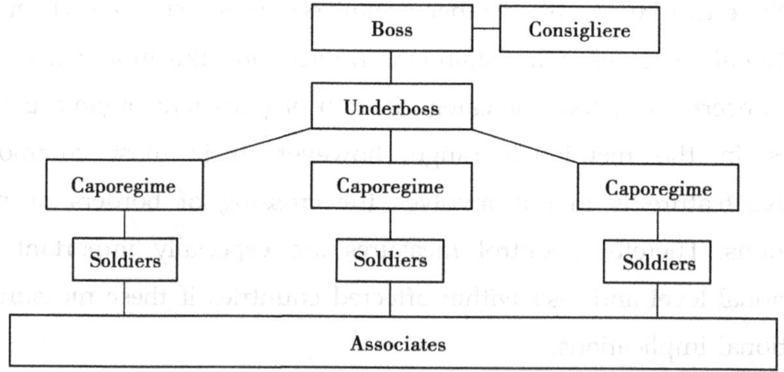

▶ Colombia Cartels (Colombia Drug Cartels)

Until 2011 Colombia remained the world's largest cocaine producer, however with a strong anti-narcotic strategy in 2012 the country achieved a great decrease in cocaine production, falling to the 3rd position, behind Peru and Bolivia. Drug cartel is a criminal organization developed with the primary purpose of promoting and controlling drug trafficking operations. They range from loosely managed agreements among various drug traffickers to formalized commercial enterprises. The term was applied when the largest trafficking organizations reached an agreement to coordinate the production and distribution of cocaine. Since that agreement was broken up, drug cartels are no longer actually cartels, but the term stuck and it is now popularly used to refer to any criminal narcotics related organization.

The current main actors in the drug trade are:

- Neo-paramilitary criminal gangs, also called BACRIM
- ELN (Weakened by a US-backed counter-insurgency plan)
- FARC (Weakened by a US-backed counter-insurgency plan)
- EPL (Partially demobilized)

Historical actors in the drug trade were:

- Cali Cartel (dissolved)
- Medellín Cartel (dismantled)
- North Coast Cartel (dismantled)
- Norte del Valle Cartel (dissolved)
- AUC (demobilized)

▶ Chinese Triads

The terms refers to many branches of Chinese underground society and/or organizations based in Hong Kong and Macau and also operating in Taiwan, mainland China, and countries and cities worldwide with significant Chinese populations such as San Francisco and Singapore. Triads also exist in Europe, South Africa, Australia, and North America. They generally follow a strict hierarchical organization of low-level gang members and office-bearers—although it is thought that no central command structure unifies the different factions within a particular Triad society. Most Triads operate largely independent of one another. In fact, it is speculated that individual office-bearers have limited control over the criminal enterprises carried out by the lower-ranking members.

Their activities include drug trafficking, contract murder, money laundering, gambling, prostitution, car theft, extortion, and other forms of racketeering. A major source of Triad income today comes from the counterfeiting of intellectual property such as clothing, computer software, music CDs and movie VCDs/DVDs. They also trade in bootleg tabacco and alcohol products.

New Words

dwarf [dwɔːf]

vt. If one person or thing is dwarfed by another, the second is so much bigger than the first that it makes them look very small. 使……显得过于矮小

E.g. His figure is dwarfed by his big brother.

adj. Dwarf is used to describe varieties or species of plants and animals which are much smaller than the usual size for their kind. (植物或动物)过于矮小的

capitalize [ˈkæpɪtlaɪz]

vi. If you capitalize on a situation, you use it to gain some advantage for yourself. 利用

E.g. The rebels seem to be trying to capitalize on the public's discontent with the government.

vt. 1) In business, if you capitalize something that belongs to you, you sell it in order to make money. [商]使资本化

E.g. Our intention is to capitalize the company by any means we can.

2) If you capitalize a letter, you write it as a capital letter. If you capitalize a word, you spell it in capital letters, or with the first letter as a capital letter. 把……大写

alliance [əˈlaɪəns]

[C] *n.* 1) An alliance is a group of countries or political parties that are formally united and working together because they have similar aims. 联盟

E.g. The two parties were still too much apart to form an alliance.

2) An alliance is a relationship in which two countries, political parties, or organizations work together for some purpose. 结盟

E.g. The Socialists' electoral strategy has been based on a tactical alliance with the Communists.

corrosive [kəˈrəʊsɪv]

adj. 1) A corrosive substance is able to destroy solid materials by a chemical reaction. 腐蚀性的

E.g. Sodium is highly corrosive.

2) If you say that something has a corrosive effect, you mean that it gradually causes serious harm. 逐渐起破坏作用的

E.g. ...the corrosive effects of rumor.

formidable [ˈfɔːmɪdəbəl]

adj. If you describe something or someone as formidable, you mean that you feel slightly frightened by them because they are very great or impressive. 可怕的;令人敬畏的

E.g. He said Mr Jones faced "formidable challenges" ranging from the economy to climate change.

criminality [ˌkrɪmɪˈnælɪti]

[U] *n.* the state or quality of being criminal 犯罪

penalty [ˈpɛnəlti]

[C] *n.* 1) A penalty is a punishment that someone is given for doing something which is against a law or rule. 刑罚

E.g. The criminal could face the death penalty.

2) In sports such as football, American football, and hockey, a penalty is

a disadvantage forced on the team that breaks a rule.（体育比赛中的）罚球

E.g. Referee had no hesitation in awarding a penalty.

3) The penalty that you pay for something you have done is something unpleasant that you experience as a result. 惩罚

E.g. Why should I pay the penalty for somebody else's mistake?

execute [ˈɛksɪkjuːt]

vt. 1) To execute someone means to kill them as a punishment for a serious crime. 处死

E.g. One group claimed to have executed the hostage.

2) If you execute a plan, you carry it out. [正式]执行(计划等)

E.g. We have plans in place and I wanted to see if the guys could execute them.

ephemeral [ɪˈfɛmərəl]

adj. If you describe something as ephemeral, you mean that it lasts only for a short time. [正式]短暂的;瞬间的

E.g. ...the ephemeral joys of childhood.

constituent [kənˈstɪtjʊənt]

[C] *n.* 1) A constituent is someone who lives in a particular constituency, especially someone who is able to vote in an election. 选民

E.g. What an easier way to prove to your constituent that you only care for them!

2) A constituent of a mixture, substance, or system is one of the things from which it is formed. 成分

E.g. Caffeine is the active constituent of drinks such as tea and coffee.

adj. The constituent parts of something are the things from which it is formed. 构成的

E.g. Memory is the important constituent part of computer system.

spectrum [ˈspɛktrəm]

[U] *n.* The spectrum is the range of different colours which is produced when light passes through a glass prism or through a drop of water. A rainbow shows the colours in the spectrum. 光谱

[C] *n.* A spectrum is a range of a particular type of thing. 范围

E.g. Even if these systems did eventually work they would not address the spectrum of related threats.

bribery [ˈbraɪbərɪ]

[U] *n.* Bribery is the act of offering someone money or something valuable in order to persuade them to do something for you. 贿赂行为

E.g. He was jailed on charges of bribery.

premeditation [prɪˌmɛdɪˈteɪʃən]

[U] *n.* Premeditation is thinking about something or planning it before you actually do it. [正式]预谋;预先策划

E.g. The judge finally concluded there was insufficient evidence of premeditation.

jurisdiction [ˌdʒʊərɪsˈdɪkʃən]

[U] *n.* Jurisdiction is the power that a court of law or an official has to carry out legal judgments or to enforce laws. 司法权;管辖权

E.g. The army and the police argued over jurisdiction rather than dispatching a rescue helicopter.

[C] *n.* A jurisdiction is a state or other area in which a particular court and system of laws has authority. [法]管辖范围

E.g. In the U.K., unlike in most other European jurisdictions, there is no right to strike.

mafia [ˈmæfɪə]

[C] *n.* 1) The Mafia is a criminal organization that makes money illegally, especially by threatening people and dealing in drugs. 黑手党

E.g. He claims that there is a sophisticated and well-organised Nigerian Mafia trafficking women into Spain.

2) You can use mafia to refer to an organized group of people who you disapprove of because they use unfair or illegal means in order to get what they want. 团伙

E.g. They are well-connected with the education-reform mafia.

cartel [kɑːˈtɛl]

[C] *n.* a group of separate companies that agree to increase profits by fixing prices and not competing with each other 卡特尔

E.g. U.S. officials say the heavily armed cartel often carries out murders, kidnappings and assaults to further its reach.

integrate [ˈɪntɪgreɪt]

vt. /vi. 1) If someone integrates into a social group, or is integrated into it, they behave in such a way that they become part of the group or are accepted into it. 使融入;结合在一起

E.g. He didn't integrate successfully into the life in Beijing.

2) When races integrate or when schools and organizations are integrated, people who belong to ethnic minorities can join others in their schools and organizations. 使合并;成为一体

E.g. The Marine Corps was the last service to integrate.

3) If you integrate one thing with another, or one thing integrates with another, the two things become closely linked or form part of a whole idea or system. You can also say that two things integrate. 结合

E.g. Writing about a topic helps you integrate new knowledge with what you already know.

sphere [sfɪə]

[C] *n.* 1) A sphere is an object that is completely round in shape like a ball. 球体

E.g. Because the earth spins, it is not a perfect sphere.

2) A sphere of activity or interest is a particular area of activity or interest. (活动、兴趣的)领域

E.g. ...the sphere of international politics.

triad [ˈtraɪæd]

[C] *n.* 1) The Triads were Chinese secret societies in old China that were often associated with organized crime. 三合会;旧中国的秘密犯罪组织

2) A triad is a group of three similar things. 三个一组

E.g. For the faculty, there exists the triad of responsibilities: teaching, research, and service.

undermine [ˌʌndəˈmaɪn]

vt. 1) If you undermine something such as a feeling or a system, you make it less strong or less secure than it was before, often by a gradual process or by repeated efforts. 逐渐削弱;逐渐动摇

E.g. Our confidence in the team has been seriously undermined by their recent defeats.

2) If you undermine someone or undermine their position or authority, you make their authority or position less secure, often by indirect methods. (通常以间接方式)动摇(某人的地位或权威)

E.g. The President's enemies are spreading rumours to undermine his authority.

3) If you undermine someone's efforts or undermine their chances of achieving something, you behave in a way that makes them less likely to succeed. 破坏;损害(某人的努力或成功的机会)

E.g. The continued fighting threatens to undermine efforts to negotiate an agreement.

democratic [ˌdɛməˈkrætɪk]

adj. 1) A democratic country, government, or political system is governed by representatives who are elected by the people. 民主的

E.g. Exercise your democratic right to vote.

2) Something that is democratic is based on the idea that everyone should have equal rights and should be involved in making important decisions. 民主精神的

E.g. a democratic decision

consolidate [kən'sɒlɪˌdeɪt]

vt. 1) If you consolidate something that you have, for example power or success, you strengthen it so that it becomes more effective or secure. 巩固

E.g. The government consolidates its power by force.

2) To consolidate a number of small groups or companies means to make them into one large organization. 合并

E.g. The Seoul government has recently consolidated several agencies to train young adults to do volunteer work in developing countries.

offset [ˌɒf'sɛt]

vt. If one thing is offset by another, the effect of the first thing is reduced by the second, so that any advantage or disadvantage is cancelled out. 抵消

E.g. Many American companies have relied on emerging-market customers to help offset weak domestic demand.

militant ['mɪlɪtənt]

adj. You use militant to describe people who believe in something very strongly and are active in trying to bring about political or social change, often in extreme ways that other people find unacceptable. 激进的

E.g. The militant wing of the Islamic group Hamas claimed responsibility for the killing of Hershkovitz.

[C] *n.* 激进分子

E.g. Those named include Saudi-born militant Osama bin Laden and several members of his family.

parasite ['pærəˌsaɪt]

[C] *n.* 1) A parasite is a small animal or plant that lives on or inside a larger animal or plant, and gets its food from it. 寄生虫；寄生植物

E.g. However, she said it was not yet clear exactly how the drugs blocked the parasite.

2) If you disapprove of someone because you think that they get money

or other things from other people but do not do anything in return, you can call them a parasite. 靠他人为生的人;寄生虫

E.g. ...a parasite, who produced nothing but lived on the work of others.

maneuver (also **manoeuvre**) [mə'nuːvə]

vt./vi. 1) If you manoeuvre something into or out of an awkward position, you skilfully move it there. (熟练地)移动

E.g. She manoeuvred the car carefully into the garage.

[U] *n.* 移动

2) If you manoeuvre a situation, you change it in a clever and skilful way so that you can benefit from it. 操控

E.g. The new laws have left us little room to manoeuvre.

[C] *n.* 操控手段

n. (*pl.*) Military manoeuvres are training exercises which involve the movement of soldiers and equipment over a large area. 演习

E.g. Allied troops begin manoeuvres tomorrow to show how quickly forces could be mobilized in case of a new invasion.

illicit [ɪ'lɪsɪt]

adj. An illicit activity or substance is not allowed by law or the social customs of a country. 违法的;不正当的

E.g. There should be some measures to prevent illicit import of weapons and ammunition into Gaza.

corruption [kə'rʌpʃən]

[U] *n.* Corruption is dishonesty and illegal behaviour by people in positions of authority or power. 腐败

E.g. The Congress has begun debating a new law to reform the police force and tackle corruption.

fauna ['fɔːnə]

[U] *n.* Animals, especially the animals in a particular area, can be referred to as fauna. (尤指某区域的)动物群

E.g. ...the flora and fauna of the African jungle.

……非洲丛林的植物群和动物群。

flora [ˈflɔːrə]

[U] *n.* You can refer to plants as flora, especially the plants growing in a particular area. (尤指某个地区的)植物群

E.g. ...the variety of food crops and flora which now exists in Dominica.

……目前存在于多米尼加的各种粮食作物和植物群。

piracy [ˈpaɪrəsɪ]

[U] *n.* 1) Piracy is robbery at sea carried out by pirates. 海盗行为

E.g. In recent years, the international community has deployed navy ships to guard the area in an effort to fight piracy.

2) You can refer to the illegal copying of things such as DVDs and computer programs as piracy. 盗版行为

E.g. ...protection against piracy of books, films, and other intellectual property.

launder [ˈlɔːndə]

vt. 1) To launder money that has been obtained illegally means to process it through a legitimate business or to send it abroad to a foreign bank, so that when it comes back nobody knows that it was illegally obtained. 洗(钱)

E.g. He's already declined an offer from someone seeking his computer skills to launder money.

2) When you launder clothes, sheets, and towels, you wash and iron them. 洗熨

E.g. freshly laundered sheets

Exercises

▶ Exercise One: Reading Comprehension

Answer the following questions in your own words after reading the passage.

1. Based on the ideas of the author, what are the essential features of transnational organized crime? Among these features, which is the key one?
2. What fact makes new transnational criminal groups essentially different from national, domestic organizations?
3. Why is it extremely difficult for law enforcement organs to get more information about the organizational structures of these groups?
4. According to the passage, what factors boost the potential of transnational criminal rings?
5. What character helps the law enforcement officers to define illicit businesses as transnational organized crime activities?

▶ Exercise Two: Translation

Please translate the following sentences into Chinese.

1. Transnational organized crime is not only a law enforcement problem, but also a formidable and increasing threat to national and international security.
2. The problem of definition is an important factor contributing to the inability of international law enforcement bodies to identify the size and scope of transnational organized crime accurately.
3. The inability of many states and international organizations to design and coordinate effective anti-criminal programs creates a favorable climate for the criminal community to maneuver in their resistance to law enforcement organs.

Part Ⅱ After-class Reading

Text B

Cooperation Types between Organized Crime Groups Around the World

Organized crime is by its very nature a transnational phenomenon. As with any of illicit goods and services must have a network of marketing, sales and distribution agents, and legitimate business, the criminal organization that wishes to compete in the international market transportation facilities and financial services in selected locations around the world. The specific characteristics of the criminal network for the commodity that is traded are established in terms of source, production, transit and target countries, and areas where profits can be hidden and/or invested. In almost every case, whether the illicit product or service be drugs, arms, counterfeit currency, illegal immigrant smuggling or the laundering of illicit profits, the process involves a cross-frontier operation, and therefore cross-frontier collaboration. In the case of cocaine, a typical chain might be as follows: the coca plant is cultivated in Peru, refined in Colombia (where the necessary precursor chemicals, manufactured elsewhere, would be assembled), sent overland to Venezuela, by sea to Spain and onwards to Italy, where, from a warehouse in Milan, it would be broken down into smaller consignments for subsequent distribution throughout western Europe. Profits would be laundered initially through finance brokerage houses in Milan, then through offshore centres in the Channel Islands or the Caribbean, and finally reinvested or repatriated.

Traditionally, there have been three distinct types of international collaboration: the first and most common is the international criminal network established by groups of a single ethnic background. Two factors have favoured this process—the speed and ease of international travel, and the multiracial diversity of modern industrialized society. The migratory flows of the twentieth century (and earlier) from poor to richer countries created large diasporas of ethnic colonies strategically scattered around the world. Links based on trust and blood relationships with the homeland and on the commercial opportunities offered by economic prosperity in the adopted country are exploited by criminals, who find cover among their predominantly law-abiding emigre compatriots. The ethnic link is particularly evident among Chinese Triad groups who tend to work almost exclusively with their own networks around the world. However, there is evidence of collaboration with other groups such as the Colombian cartels for cocaine smuggling and with the Italian Mafia, primarily for the purpose of illegal alien smuggling.

The second form of collaboration consists of *ad hoc* arrangements between sellers and buyers, where deals are negotiated through recognized intermediaries in the various illicit markets. Typical of these would be the trade of opium gum or morphine base between local producers and traffickers in the Golden Crescent (Afghanistan, Pakistan, Iran) or in the Middle East, or arms deals negotiated by or for organized crime groups in a West African city. In such cases, buyers and sellers meet in neutral territory where the nationality of the intermediaries is unimportant, and where the only criteria for doing business are an agreement on terms between buyer and seller and a climate which permits illicit deals and transportation to be effected with a minimum of disturbance from law enforcement authorities or inquisitive officialdom. With this type of collaboration, buyers and sellers need not be affiliated members of an organized crime group, merely unscrupulous entrepreneurs willing to take the risk of transacting business in a market where the only form of contract enforcement is the threat or use of violence. The bartering of drugs for arms or for money to buy arms is a common feature, not only of collaboration between organized crime groups but also of that between organized crime groups and terrorist organizations, as has been the case in Peru and Colombia, and between organized crime groups and insurgent nationalist or religious groups, as in Afghanistan, Sri Lanka, Kosovo and Burma.

A third form of international cooperation derives from chance contacts or meetings between individual criminals and organized crime groups which lead on to a more stable relationship. Important supply lines of morphine base and heroin to the Sicilian Mafia, Cosa Nostra, were set up in the late 1970s and early 1980s after Cosa Nostra members Pietro Vernengo and Gaspare Mutolo shared prison cells in Italy with the Turkish trafficker, Yasar Aunoi Mussullulu, and the Singapore-born Chinese, Koh Bak Kin, respectively. Sicilian judges estimate that between 1981 and 1983, Mussullulu alone supplied two Mafia individuals with two metric tons of morphine base for the sum of 55 million U.S. dollars, after which he disappeared from circulation and his supply line to Italy ceased. Koh Bak Kin was first arrested at Rome airport in 1976 with more than 20 kilograms of heroin and in 1978 was sentenced to six years in prison. The already lenient sentence was further reduced, and Kin was released from prison in 1980. On his return to Bangkok, he was able to guarantee a steady supply of heroin to Cosa Nostra thanks to his links in northern Thailand with an emissary of the opium "baron" Khun Sa. He was re-arrested in 1983 at Suez, aboard a Greek ship which was carrying 233 kilos of pure heroin to Sicily.

While all three forms of collaboration—shared ethnicity networks, "ad hoc" arrangements and "contingency factor" deals have continued—a significant new type of alliance has been created in the course of the last decade, the "strategic partnership". Strategic partnerships break new ground in two important ways: firstly, they show a shift from collaborating networks of a single ethnic group dispersed over different continents towards a collaboration between organized crime groups of different nationalities and ethnic backgrounds; secondly, these alliances are neither contingent nor ad hoc but represent an embryonic form of federalisation—that is, strategic alliances, which are reasonably stable in time and are forged on the basis of congruent goals. Strategic partnerships have the same function as their counterpart agreements in legitimate business—to spread and reduce risk and to gain market access.

The emergence of strategic partnerships is not simply the outcome of criminal minds at work, but owes much to the profound economic and geo-political changes which have taken place over the last decade. Even more efficiently than legal operators, organized crime groups have been quick to take advantage of new opportunities: they have exploited the internationalization of legal, commercial and financial markets, the relaxation of international boundaries, scientific and technological advances—particularly in the field of telecommunications—and new geo-political configurations around the world. Taken together, these elements have encouraged the internationalization and progressive integration of criminal markets in goods and services, which now appear regulated by consent, rather than by violent power struggles, into sectoral and geographical areas of competence. This has occurred at national level in Italy, where instead of competing for the same markets, a kind of "syndication" of the four major organized crime groups—Cosa Nostra, the Camorra (from the Naples area), the "Ndrangheta" (Calabria) and the United Holy Crown (Apulia)—has taken place. Where once these groups fought for market shares, nowadays when they operate outside their home regions they divide up territory and activities without undue conflict, while services such as money laundering tend to be centralized in the hands of professional outsiders. The same pattern has also developed at international level.

The current structure of the strategic partnership has been determined largely by two forms of criminal expansion—the flow of CIS criminals to Western Europe and North America and the counter-wave of West European and South American criminal organizations to the countries of the former Soviet Union, with the mafia organizations fast emerging as the key players. Just as any operation involving the international movement of cocaine has traditionally involved dealing directly with the Colombian cartels, organized criminals in every continent must now reckon on having to do business with the Russians.

(1, 285 words)

Unit 2

Terrorism

Part Ⅰ In-class Reading

Pre-reading Questions

- *Please share your own understanding of the text with your classmates.*
- *Please figure out your own answers to the questions proposed by the author in the end of the text.*

Text A

Evolving Terrorist Threat

Long-term Trends and Drivers and Their Implications for Emergency Management

Overview

There are several ways that terrorist tactics are likely to evolve in the coming decades:

- Terrorists may favor attack methods that exploit perceived vulnerabilities, such as adopting active shooter tactics and finding new methods of concealing dangerous materials.
- Terrorists will continue to pursue opportunities to inflict mass

casualties.

- The nature of the threat from international Islamic terrorist groups is likely to change, particularly considering the Arab Spring and death of Osama bin Laden.
- Homegrown violent extremism will likely continue to emerge as a significant threat.

Key Trends and Drivers

Terrorist tactics may shift to exploit vulnerabilities, including those against active shooter-type attacks and screening for concealed weapons. Terrorist tactics tend to favor attacks that avoid effective countermeasures and exploit vulnerabilities. For example, recent suicide operations have targeted countries' lack of experience and capability to respond to simultaneous and well resourced attacks, like those in Mumbai, or suicide shooters, like the Fort Hood attack. Both of those attacks featured tactics that resemble "active shooters", a situation which police are generally trained to cordon off an area and wait for paramilitary response units, like SWAT teams. In Mumbai, this paradigm was exploited by terrorists who laid siege to entire areas, carried supplies to extend the length of time they could operate, and attacked response teams.

These sorts of attack methods have lower consequences than catastrophic chemical, biological, radiological, or nuclear (CBRN) attacks or improvised explosive device attacks, but have a higher probability of succeeding. In addition, these types of tactics are hard to distinguish from traditional disasters. Responders to the first World Trade Center attack and Oklahoma City Bombing believed they were responding to accidents, while responders to plane crashes in New York City since September 11 have believed they were responding to terrorist incidents. Responding to conventional terrorist attacks can also be complicated for first responders, due to the possibility that secondary devices may be targeted at them.

An additional tactic that terrorists have adopted to exploit vulnerabilities is to find new, seemingly innocuous places to conceal weapons, explosives, and other dangerous materials. Richard Reid concealed explosives in his shoes in December 2001, terrorists planned to conceal liquid explosives in soft drink containers, Umar Farouk Amdulmutallab concealed explosives hidden in his underwear in December 2009, and bombs were found in toner cartridges flown from Yemen in October 2010. In each case, screening and other countermeasures were altered to try to reduce their vulnerabilities to these types of attacks. Drug smugglers and customs enforcers have engaged in a similar process where concealment methods evolve as new countermeasures are put in place. As terrorist concealment tactics evolve, this may force emergency managers and first responders to reconsider screening procedures during special events.

Terrorist groups will still pursue opportunities to inflict mass casualties. For example, terrorists continued to target commercial aircraft despite the employment of enhanced security measures at airports. The tactics favored by terrorists have become more lethal over time, a trend which could continue. The proliferation of advanced technologies throughout the world will provide terrorist groups with easier access to CBRN weapons, as well as to advanced conventional weapons. However, some experts said terrorist groups are unlikely to deploy CBRN weapons successfully, pointing to failed attempts to do so in the past and a current preference to employ conventional weapons.

An increase in the number of terrorist attacks, or the successful deployment of a CBRN device, may also result in a decreased focus on natural hazards. During the Cold War, FEMA concentrated more than three-quarters of its resources on preparing for a nuclear attack, which reduced preparedness for natural disasters. After the September 11 attacks, the Federal government deemphasized the role of FEMA and focused emergency management funding toward responding to terrorist attacks. The report of the Select Bipartisan Committee to Investigate the Preparation and Response to Hurricane Katrina suggested that this focus on terrorism may have negatively affected preparedness efforts focused on other hazards.

Global Islamic terrorism may not continue to be the primary terrorist threat to the United States. According to the National Intelligence Council, the history of other terrorist threats suggests that Islamic terrorist groups may become less significant or even dissolve over the next few decades. Previous terrorist waves (anarchists in the late-19th and early-20th centuries, anti-colonial insurgents in the early-20th Century, and New Left terrorists in the mid-20th Century) lasted about 40 years. The nature of al-Qaeda makes it particularly susceptible to subside as a significant threat. Two key factors that contribute to the longevity—achieving strategic objectives and transitioning to become a legitimate political group—are unlikely because the group's objectives are to establish a global Islamic caliphate and topple Western-influenced regimes in the Middle East.

The "Arab Spring" uprisings in the Middle East and the death of Osama bin Laden will have significant influences on global Islamic terrorism. There is a considerable amount of uncertainty regarding the impact of these events. Some regimes in the Middle East have supported the United States in suppressing Islamic terrorism, but also have been accused of not doing enough or even tacitly supporting terrorist groups. There were concerns that new regimes in Arab countries could be friendlier to Islamic extremism, but there are also some who believe the opposite will be true. Similarly, there were concerns that the death of bin Laden may spur reprisals as well as assertions that al-Qaeda was permanently weakened with his death.

Homegrown violent extremists are a growing source of concern. The number of cases where American citizens or permanent residents were radicalized and recruited to participate in Islamic terrorist activities increased sharply in 2009. The Federal response to homegrown violent extremism is difficult, because the legal authority of some Federal counterterrorism tools, particularly those employed by the Department of Defense and the Intelligence Community, may not allow them to be employed against American citizens. Additionally, there is a continuing but low-level threat from other domestic sources of terrorism. Between 2008 and 2009, there were 12 successful terrorist attacks in the United States, only three of which were linked to Islamic extremism. The others were linked to groups with agendas focused on abortion, animal rights, the environment, or white supremacy.

The possibility of domestic terrorism could divert attention and/or resources from natural hazards. The Bipartisan Policy Center recommended that a Federal agency like the Department of Homeland Security be tasked with identifying radicalization and interdicting recruitment of U.S. citizens and residents. In addition, multiple reports recommended further engaging State and local public safety officials, particularly police organizations, in countering terrorist threats.

Correlation to Other Drivers

• Changing Role of the Individual: A significant trend in this area is individuals affiliating with communities of like-minded people. This may facilitate the radicalization of American citizens. According to a report from the Homeland Security Institute, "the Internet plays a vital role in creating social bonds that are necessary for radicalization and recruitment, as well as providing a venue for perpetuating radicalization among groups of recruits." This includes individuals who "self-radicalize" by seeking out terrorist organizations. Experts have raised concerns about the possibility that terrorist attacks perpetrated by radicalized Americans may be more successful and lethal due to terrorist organizations' ability to connect to radicalized Americans remotely and provide resources and suggested tactics.

• Global Interdependencies: Globalization has increased the reach of transnational organizations. As global connections continue to expand, the reach of these organizations will also have the opportunity to expand. Additionally, globalization has allowed terrorist organizations to become largely independent of former state sponsors.

• Technological Innovation and Dependency: Technological innovation is a double-edged sword in the world of terrorism. Networked video cameras, nanotechnology, and software designed to identify important intelligence information could become powerful tools for counterterrorism operations, increasing the effectiveness of antiterrorism countermeasures. However, terrorists will also benefit from technological innovation. The diffusion of advanced technological capabilities could facilitate their access to CBRN materials, as well as advanced technologies such as guided missiles. Advanced technologies could also increase terrorist groups' access to radicalized American citizens.

• Universal Access to and Use of Information: During the Mumbai terrorist attacks, social networking websites Twitter and Flickr were initially reporting the events more quickly than western news outlets. This raised several concerns, including public access to gruesome news and images, as well as the possibility that terrorists conducting the attack were able to follow the actions of emergency responders through Twitter.

Conclusions & Questions

Shifting attack methods may require emergency managers and first responders to alter response tactics. How will first responders prevent themselves from becoming additional casualties during active terrorist events? How will the public respond if terrorist adopted active shooter-type tactics?

Terrorism competes with natural hazards for emergency management resources and attention. Would the response to successful terrorist attacks reduce preparedness for other hazards? Alternatively, would a perceived decrease in the threat from terrorism reduce the homeland security resources available to emergency managers?

Islamic extremism is likely to change significantly over the next 15 years. Will the Arab Spring and Osama bin Laden's death increase, decrease, or not influence Islamic extremists' desire and capability to attack the United States?

The threat of domestic terrorism may result in increased counterterrorism responsibilities for state and local emergency managers and partners. How will the roles of emergency managers and first responders change as their counterterrorism responsibilities increase? How will the Federal government's relationship with state and local emergency managers change? What will be the distinction between law enforcement activities and counterterrorism activities? Will this lead to the "militarization" of law enforcement?

Social and technological changes will significantly affect the character of the terrorist threat. Will terrorist groups or counterterrorism organizations benefit more from advancing technology? How should emergency managers and first responders treat the possibility of attacks using CBRN weapons? What are the implications to emergency managers and first responders if more American citizens and residents participate in terrorist attacks?

Background Information

▶ the Fort Hood attack

On November 5, 2009, a mass murder took place at Fort Hood, near Killeen, Texas. Nidal Malik Hasan, a U.S. Army major and psychiatrist, fatally shot 13 people and injured more than 30 others. The shooting produced more casualties than any other on an American military base.

On April 2, 2014, a shooting spree occurred at several locations on the Fort Hood military base near Killeen, Texas. Four people, including the gunman, were killed, while sixteen additional people were injured. The shooter, 34-year-old Ivan Lopez, died of a self-inflicted gunshot wound.

▶ FEMA

FEMA (Federal Emergency Management Agency) is an agency of the United States Department of Homeland Security. The agency's primary purpose is to coordinate the response to a disaster that has occurred in the United States and that overwhelms the resources of local and state authorities. The governor of the state in which the disaster occurs must declare a state of emergency and formally request from the president that FEMA and the federal government respond to the disaster. FEMA also provides these services for territories of the United States.

New Words

tactic [ˈtæktɪk]

[C] *n.* Tactics are the methods that you choose to use in order to achieve what you want in a particular situation. 战术

E.g. The rebels would still be able to use guerrilla tactics to make the country ungovernable.

evolve [ɪˈvɒlv]

vi. When animals or plants evolve, they gradually change and develop into different forms. 进化

E.g. The three species evolved from a single ancestor.

vt./vi. If something evolves or you evolve it, it gradually develops over a period of time into something different and usually more advanced. 使……逐步发展;逐步发展

E.g. The company has evolved into a major chemical manufacturer.

exploit *v.* [ɪkˈsplɔɪt] *n.* [ˈɛksplɔɪt]

vt. 1) If you say that someone is exploiting you, you think that they are treating you unfairly by using your work or ideas and giving you very little in return. 利用;剥削

E.g. The company exploited those young employees for great profits.

2) If you say that someone is exploiting a situation, you disapprove of them because they are using it to gain an advantage for themselves, rather than trying to help other people or do what is right. [表不满]利用(某种情势)

E.g. The government and its opponents compete to exploit the troubles to their advantage.

3) If you exploit something, you use it well, and achieve something or gain an advantage from it. 充分利用

E.g. Teachers should be exploiting computers in education.

4) To exploit resources or raw materials means to develop them and use them for industry or commercial activities. 开发利用(资源、原材料)

E.g. Turkey says neither side of the island should exploit energy resources until reunification talks are complete.

vulnerable [ˈvʌlnərəbəl]

adj. 1) Someone who is vulnerable is weak and without protection, with the result that they are easily hurt physically or emotionally. 易受伤害的

E.g. Women and children are particularly vulnerable members of our society.

→派生词 vulnerability [U] *n.*

E.g. Now that we know the basis of an attack, what can we do to protect ourselves from this vulnerability?

2) If a person, animal, or plant is vulnerable to a disease, they are more likely to get it than other people, animals, or plants. 容易患……病的

E.g. People with high blood pressure are especially vulnerable to diabetes.

→派生词 vulnerability [U] *n.* 患病的可能性

E.g. Taking long-term courses of certain medicines may increase vulnerability to infection.

conceal [kən'siːl]

vt. 1) If you conceal something, you cover it or hide it carefully. 掩盖;隐藏

E.g. Traffickers also recently attempted to conceal 80 kg of heroin in sacks of red chilli powder.

2) If you conceal a piece of information or a feeling, you do not let other people know about it. 隐瞒(信息);掩饰(情感)

E.g. Maggie, on the other hand, tried to conceal her misery by making other people laugh.

inflict [ɪn'flɪkt]

vt. To inflict harm or damage on someone or something means to make them suffer it. 使遭受(伤害或破坏等)

E.g. We have worked closely with partners, including Yemen, to inflict major blows against al-Qaeda leaders.

casualty ['kæʒjʊəltɪ]

[C] *n.* 1) A casualty is a person who is injured or killed in a war or in an accident. 死伤者

E.g. At the current daily casualty rate, officials said, medical supplies will run out in two weeks.

2) A casualty of a particular event or situation is a person or a thing that has suffered badly as a result of that event or situation. 受害者

E.g. The car industry has been one of the greatest casualties of the recession.

countermeasure ['kaʊntəˌmɛʒə]

[C] *n.* A countermeasure is an action that you take in order to weaken the effect of another action or a situation, or to make it harmless. 对策;对抗措施

E.g. The country had already taken effective countermeasures to fight terrorism.

simultaneous [ˌsɪməl'teɪnɪəs]

adj. Things which are simultaneous happen or exist at the same time. 同时的

E.g. Any ceasefire would be simultaneous with the withdrawal of U.S. forces.

resemble [rɪˈzɛmbəl]

vt. If one thing or person resembles another, they are similar to each other. 像

E.g. She closely resembles her sister.

cordon [ˈkɔːdən]

[C] *n.* A cordon is a line or ring of police, soldiers, or vehicles preventing people from entering or leaving an area. 警戒线

E.g. More than 1,000 people, mostly youths, shouted their rage, kept back by the cordon and police officers.

paramilitary [ˌpærəˈmɪlɪtərɪ]

adj. A paramilitary organization is organized like an army and performs either civil or military functions in a country. (组织)准军事性的

E.g. Military helicopters are circling the city carrying heavily armed paramilitary police.

[C] *n.* Paramilitaries are members of a paramilitary organization. 准军事组织成员

E.g. Paramilitaries and army recruits patrolled the village.

adj. A paramilitary organization is an illegal group that is organized like an army. 非法军事组织的

E.g. The agency begins its work two days after Northern Ireland's largest paramilitary group announced a year-long ceasefire.

[C] *n.* Paramilitaries are members of an illegal paramilitary organization. 非法军事组织成员

E.g. Paramilitaries were blamed for the shooting.

paradigm [ˈpærəˌdaɪm]

[C] *n.* A paradigm is a model for something that explains it or shows how it can be produced. 范例

E.g. We can foresee a new paradigm in the global market in the 21st century.

catastrophic [ˌkætəˈstrɒfɪk]

adj. 1) Something that is catastrophic involves or causes a sudden terrible disaster. 灾难性的

E.g. A tidal wave caused by the earthquake hit the coast causing catastrophic damage.

2) If you describe something as catastrophic, you mean that it is very bad or unsuccessful. 极糟的;失败的

E.g. For the government, it is another catastrophic attempt to rescue the economy.

radiological [ˌreɪdɪəˈlɒdʒɪkəl]

adj. 1) Radiological means relating to radiology. 放射医学的

E.g. ...patients subjected to extensive radiological examinations.

……接受全面放射检查的病人。

2) Radiological means relating to radioactive materials. 放射材料的

E.g. ... the National Radiological Protection Board's guidelines for storing nuclear waste.

……国家放射性材料保护委员会关于存放核废料的指导原则。

improvise [ˈɪmprəˌvaɪz]

vt. /vi. 1) If you improvise, you make or do something using whatever you have or without having planned it in advance. 临时拼凑

E.g. He worked late into the night and improvised a meal for himself.

2) When performers improvise, they invent music or words as they play, sing, or speak. 即兴演奏;即席演说

E.g. His grandfather noticed that he would often improvise melodies as he played with his toys.

innocuous [ɪˈnɒkjʊəs]

adj. Something that is innocuous is not at all harmful or offensive. 无害的;无意冒犯的

E.g. But the seemingly innocuous message also has the potential to assist cyberthieves in stealing your identity.

cartridge [ˈkɑːtrɪdʒ]

[C]*n.* 1) A cartridge is a metal or cardboard tube containing a bullet and an explosive substance. Cartridges are used in guns. 弹药筒

E.g. Only five of the seven spent cartridges were recovered by police.

2) A cartridge is part of a machine or device that can be easily removed and replaced when it is worn out or empty. (机器或装置中可替换的部分)套筒

smuggle [ˈsmʌgəl]

vt. If someone smuggles things or people into a place or out of it, they take them there illegally or secretly. 走私;偷运

E.g. Sophisticated new techniques have been developed to smuggle drugs, according to crime expert Kenny Simpson.

→派生词 smuggling [U]*n.* 走私

lethal [ˈliːθəl]

adj. 1) A substance that is lethal can kill people or animals. 致命的

E.g. a lethal weapon

2) If you describe something as lethal, you mean that it is capable of causing a lot of damage. 危害极大的

E.g. You and that car—it's a lethal combination.

proliferation [prəˌlifəˈreiʃən]

[U]*n.* the sudden increase in the number or amount of sth.; a large number of a particular thing 增殖;扩散;激增

E.g. (1)...attempts to prevent cancer cell proliferation.

(2)...a proliferation of personal computers.

anarchist [ˈænəkɪst]

[C]*n.* An anarchist is a person who believes in anarchism. 无政府主义者

E.g. Some anarchist and anti-globalization groups have also threatened to protest in London during the day of the wedding.

adj. If someone has anarchist beliefs or views, they believe in anarchism. 无政

府主义的

E.g. Police must be alert to a range of threats, from anarchist protesters to Irish republican terrorists to al-Qaeda-inspired extremists.

insurgent [ɪnˈsɜːdʒənt]

[C] *n.* Insurgents are people who are fighting against the government or army of their own country. 起义者,反叛者

E.g. an attack by armed insurgents

susceptible [səˈsɛptəbəl]

adj. 1) If you are susceptible to something or someone, you are very likely to be influenced by them. 易受……影响的

E.g. Young people are the most susceptible to advertisements.

2) If you are susceptible to a disease or injury, you are very likely to be affected by it. 易受(伤)的;易患(病)的

E.g. Walking with weights makes the shoulders very susceptible to injury.

subside [səbˈsaɪd]

vi. 1) If a feeling or noise subsides, it becomes less strong or loud. 减弱

E.g. I took an aspirin and the pain gradually subsided.

2) If fighting subsides, it becomes less intense or general. 平息

E.g. The tensions provoked by this remarkable contest will subside.

3) If the ground or a building is subsiding, it is very slowly sinking to a lower level. 下陷

E.g. Does that mean the whole house is subsiding?

4) If a level of water, especially flood water, subsides, it goes down. (尤指洪水的水位)回落

E.g. Energy Minister Pichai Naripthaphan said, however, that floods may finally begin to subside in the capital by mid-November, according to a government statement late Monday.

legitimate [lɪˈdʒɪtɪmɪt]

adj. 1) Something that is legitimate is acceptable according to the law. 合法的

E.g. In doing so, the unauthorized user could change the password and effectively lock legitimate users out.

2) If you say that something such as a feeling or claim is legitimate, you think that it is reasonable and justified. 合理的

E.g. That's a perfectly legitimate fear.

regime [rɪˈʒiːm, reɪ-]

[C] *n.* 1) If you refer to a government or system of running a country as a regime, you are critical of it because you think it is not democratic and uses unacceptable methods. [表不满]统治

E.g. "Let's not lose sight that it is the Gadhafi regime which started this crisis," Bracken said.

2) A regime is the way that something such as an institution, company, or economy is run, especially when it involves tough or severe action. (机构、公司或经济等的)管理方式

E.g. Our tax regime is one of the most favourable in Europe.

spur [spɜː]

vt. 1) If one thing spurs you to do another, it encourages you to do it. 鼓动;激励

E.g. Some believe that making security more pleasant will help spur more people to travel.

2) If something spurs a change or an event, it makes it happen faster or sooner. [新闻]使更快发生;加速

E.g. For Japan, he urges a major expansion of money supply, to fight deflation and spur spending.

[C] *n.* Something that acts as a spur to something else encourages a person or organization to do that thing or makes it happen more quickly. 促进因素;推动

E.g. They thought that competition can be a spur to efficiency.

reprisal [rɪˈpraɪzəl]

[C] *n.* If you do something to a person in reprisal, you hurt or punish them because they have done something violent or unpleasant to you. 报复

E.g. There is substantial evidence to suggest the Syrian regime carried out reprisal attacks against al-Harmoush's family.

assert [əˈsɜːt]

vt. 1) If someone asserts a fact or belief, they state it firmly. 坚定地陈述

E.g. (1) Mr. Helm plans to assert that the bill violates the First Amendment.

赫尔姆先生计划坚定地陈述该法案有违《第一修正案》。

(2) The defendants, who continue to assert their innocence, are expected to appeal.

那些继续宣称其清白的被告预计会上诉。

2) If you assert your authority, you make it clear by your behaviour that you have authority. 显示(权威)

E.g. The army made an attempt to assert its authority in the country.

3) If you assert your right or claim to something, you insist that you have the right to it. 坚持(权利或要求)

E.g. It's not the first time the Navajo Nation has taken action to assert its trademarks.

4) If you assert yourself, you speak and act in a forceful way, so that people take notice of you. 彰显(自己)

E.g. And they are beginning to find the confidence that is necessary to assert themselves and their identity.

radicalize [ˈrædɪkəˌlaɪz]

vt./vi. If something radicalizes a process, situation, or person, it makes them more radical. 使激进化

E.g. Across the Muslim world, government attempts to suppress Islamic groups and parties have served only to radicalize them.

supremacy [səˈpreməsi]

[U] *n.* ~(over sb./sth.) (written) a position in which you have more power, authority or status than anyone else （力量、权威等）至高无上

E.g. (1) the battle for supremacy in the region

(2) The company has established total supremacy over its rivals.

interdict [ˈɪntədikt]

vt. If an armed force interdicts something or someone, they stop them and prevent them from moving. If they interdict a route, they block it or cut it off. 阻断；封锁

E.g. Troops could be ferried in to interdict drug shipments.

affiliate *N.* [əˈfɪliˌɪt] *V.* [əˈfɪliˌeɪt]

[C] *n.* An affiliate is an organization which is officially connected with another, larger organization or is a member of it. 分支机构；成员组织

E.g. Officials believe Yemen's al-Qaeda affiliate could be strengthened by its new ties with al-Shabaab.

vi. If an organization affiliates with another larger organization, it forms a close connection with the larger organization or becomes a member of it. 成为隶属机构；成为会员组织

E.g. He wanted to affiliate with the firm because he needed expert advice in legal affairs.

gruesome [ˈgruːsəm]

adj. Something that is gruesome is extremely unpleasant and shocking. 可怕的

E.g. There has been a series of gruesome murders in this city.

Exercises

▶ Exercise One: Reading comprehension

Answer the following questions in your own words after reading the passage.

1. In the passage, the author mentioned that terrorists may favor attack methods that exploit perceived vulnerabilities. So could you introduce some tactics the terrorist have adopted to exploit vulnerabilities?
2. Compared with the catastrophic chemical, biological, radiological, or nuclear (CBRN) attacks or the improvised explosive device attacks, could you conclude the advantages of the attack methods that exploit perceived vulnerabilities?
3. Could you list the reasons why the author has the idea that the Federal response to homegrown violent extremism is difficult?
4. According to the passage, what are the advantages and disadvantages brought by technological innovation when combating terrorism?

▶ Exercise Two: Translation

Please translate the following sentences into Chinese.

1. For example, recent suicide operations have targeted countries' lack of experience and capability to respond to simultaneous and well resourced attacks, like those in Mumbai, or suicide shooters, like the Fort Hood attack.
2. There were concerns that new regimes in Arab countries could be friendlier to Islamic extremism, but there are also some who believe the opposite will be true. Similarly, there were concerns that the death of bin Laden may spur reprisals as well as assertions that al-Qaeda was permanently weakened with his death.
3. The Federal response to homegrown violent extremism is difficult, because the legal authority of some Federal counterterrorism tools, particularly those employed by the Department of Defense and the Intelligence Community, may not allow them to be employed against American citizens.

4. Experts have raised concerns about the possibility that terrorist attacks perpetrated by radicalized Americans may be more successful and lethal due to terrorist organizations' ability to connect to radicalized Americans remotely and provide resources and suggested tactics.
5. Networked video cameras, nanotechnology, and software designed to identify important intelligence information could become powerful tools for counterterrorism operations, increasing the effectiveness of antiterrorism countermeasures. However, terrorists will also benefit from technological innovation. The diffusion of advanced technological capabilities could facilitate their access to CBRN materials, as well as advanced technologies such as guided missiles. Advanced technologies could also increase terrorist groups' access to radicalized American citizens.

Part Ⅱ After-class Reading

Text B

WITS Database of Terrorist Incidents in the United States

WITS is the U.S. government's unclassified, authoritative database on terrorist incidents. Initiated in 2004, WITS collects data from a wide selection of international and domestic open sources and catalogs terrorist attacks into the database. This statistical information is posted onto NCTC's website on a quarterly basis for public view.

The Methodology Used to Compile the WITS Database of Terrorist Incidents

In order to track terrorism, a clear definition must be provided to ensure objective and consistent recording. WITS uses the U.S.C. definition of terrorism as the guiding mechanism for the database. Title 22, Section 2656f-(d)[2] of the U.S.C. provides that terrorism is "premeditated, politically motivated violence perpetrated against noncombatant targets by subnational groups or clandestine agents." This U.S.C. definition of terrorism is the cornerstone of WITS data entry and an incident must meet the provided criteria to be entered into the database.

A methodology was established to systematically process the vast amount of open source information collected by WITS. From 2007 to 2009, annual methodology conferences comprised of analysts and academia were conducted as a rigorous exercise in collaboration and evaluation to establish sound counting rules and processes to collect and code information for WITS. The result of the collaboration was a methodology that permits both expansive searches and credible results.

Terrorists, under the WITS methodology, must have initiated and executed an attack for the attack to be included in the database. Specifically, the incident must have resulted in some sort of active, kinetic effect—such as an explosion or inflicted injury or damage. Failed or foiled attacks, hoaxes, spontaneous hate crimes, and genocide are not included.

The WITS database contains over 85,000 incidents. More than 90 search fields are in the database to facilitate productive and independent searches by the user. Key fields, including "event", "victim", and "perpetrator types", provide details about the nature of cataloged terrorist incidents.

Event types cataloged in WITS include, but are not limited to, armed attack, kidnapping, bombing, and assault. Some coding is straight forward, other coding practices are more involved. For instance, incidents involving mortars, rockets, and rocket-propelled grenades are coded as armed attacks, not bombings, because they employ fired weapons. Attacks using improvised explosive devices (IEDs) and vehicle-borne IEDs (VBIEDs) are coded in a distinct category under bombing to indicate when altered, adapted, or homemade munitions were utilized. Information about suicide events is also captured.

Victim types cataloged in WITS include, but are not limited to, civilians, business people, students, military, and police. Victims' nationalities are also recorded in WITS where open source media reports such information. The methodology presumes most victims to be local nationals unless otherwise reported in the press.

Perpetrator information is included in WITS, but under select criteria. A group will be included in WITS only if it has been designated as a Foreign Terrorist Organization by the Department of State, if it has claimed status as a terrorist group or responsibility for terrorist acts, or if it has been repeatedly and reliably suspected of terrorist activity. When reporting provides detailed information, a confidence level as to the identity of the perpetrator of "likely", "plausible", or "unlikely" can be cataloged. NCTC may also infer the identity of a perpetrator, when none is identified, in instances where only one group is active in the particular region in question or the various attack characteristics match the *modus operandi* of a single group.

In order to be more analytically useful, the database also provides specification with respect to the impact of attacks. For instance, killed, wounded, and kidnapped figures are provided with as much detail as possible. In addition, targeting characteristics are coded that register violence that appears to target certain groups, including cultural, ethnic, or religious groups. Where facilities have been attacked, damage estimates are listed as Light ($1 to $500 thousand), Moderate ($500 thousand to $20 million), or Heavy (over $20 million).

Determining when noncombatants have been targeted, as provided in the U. S. C. definition, can be challenging. NCTC developed a combatant matrix that details the various areas of war-like settings and the common combatant or combatant-like actors such as military police, militias, and soldiers. NCTC utilizes this combatant matrix to determine when an act targeting combatant-like actors should be included in WITS. To remain as accurate as possible, the combatant matrix is adjusted when circumstances surrounding world conflicts change.

In the cases of Iraq and Afghanistan, it can be difficult to gather comprehensive information about all attacks. For instance, distinguishing terrorism from other forms of violence, such as sectarian violence in Iraq, is usually complex. In addition, over the past year, there was a noted decline in open source reporting in Afghanistan. Due to these conditions, the WITS dataset likely undercounts the number of attacks in Iraq and Afghanistan for 2011.

It is important that readers of this report recognize that it is based on data collected through the distinct methodology employed by WITS. Other institutions and parties processing statistical terrorism data may employ methodologies that yield different results. In addition, while reviewing the NRT, readers are encouraged to study all statistical categories presented to gain a more balanced perspective on global terrorist events as they occurred. With that in mind, the statistical information provided in the NRT is a comprehensive source of information on terrorism incidents for 2011 and can serve as valuable reference.

NCTC Observations on the Statistical Material Provided by WITS

Over 10,000 terrorist attacks occurred in 2011, affecting nearly 45,000 victims in 70 countries and resulting in over 12,500 deaths. The total number of worldwide attacks in 2011, however, dropped by almost 12 percent from 2010 and nearly 29 percent from 2007. Although the 2011 numbers represent five-year lows, they also underscore the human toll and geographic reach of terrorism. The Near East and South Asia continued to experience the most attacks, incurring just over 75 percent of the 2011 total. In addition, Africa and the Western Hemisphere experienced five-year highs in the number of attacks, exhibiting the constant evolution of the terrorist threat.

Sunni extremists accounted for the greatest number of terrorist attacks and fatalities for the third consecutive year. More than 5,700 incidents were attributed to Sunni extremists, accounting for nearly 56 percent of all attacks and about 70 percent of all fatalities. Among this perpetrator group, al-Qa'ida (AQ) and its affiliates were responsible for at least 688 attacks that resulted in almost 2,000 deaths, while the Taliban in Afghanistan and Pakistan conducted over 800 attacks that resulted in nearly 1,900 deaths. Secular, political, and anarchist groups were the next largest category of perpetrators, conducting 2,283 attacks with 1,926 fatalities, a drop of 5 percent and 9 percent, respectively, from 2010.

• Attacks by AQ and its affiliates increased by 8 percent from 2010 to 2011. A significant increase in attacks by al-Shabaab, from 401 in 2010 to 544 in 2011, offset a sharp decline in attacks by al-Qa'ida in Iraq (AQI) and a smaller decline in attacks by al-Qa'ida in the Arabian Peninsula (AQAP) and al-Qa'ida in the Islamic Maghreb (AQIM).

• The most active of the secular, political, and anarchist groups in 2011 included the FARC (377 attacks), the Communist Party of India-Maoist (CPI-Maoist) (351 attacks), the New People's Army/Communist Party of the Philippines (NPA-CPP) (102 attacks), and the Kurdistan Worker's Party (PKK) in Turkey (48 attacks).

Notable 2011 Sunni Extremist Attacks Cataloged in WITS:

• On June 3, in Sanaa, Yemen, suspected AQAP members bombed the Presidential Palace, injuring President Ali Abdallah Salih and Prime Minister Ali Muhammad Mujawar, and killing and injuring 16 members of their entourage and bodyguards. This was the only attack in 2011 where a sitting head of state was wounded.

• On August 26, in Abuja, Nigeria, Boko Haram conducted its first attack against a foreign target with a suicide Vehicle-Borne Improvised

Explosive Device (VBIED) attack on the United Nations compound in Abuja, Nigeria, killing 12 UN staff members and 12 others and wounding 115 persons. This is the largest terrorist attack in the country to date.

- On September 20, in Kabul, Afghanistan, a suspected Taliban suicide bomber detonated an Improvised Explosive Device (IED) at the residence of the former President of Afghanistan and current Peace Council Chief, killing the Peace Council Chief and five others and wounding several civilians.

- On October 4, in Mogadishu, Somalia, a suspected al-Shabaab suicide bomber drove a truck into a government compound and detonated a VBIED, killing 91 civilians and nine children and wounding 164 civilians and children. This incident resulted in the most total victims of any single attack during 2011.

Other Notable Attacks Cataloged in WITS:

- On March 13, in Nzako, Central African Republic, suspected Lord's Resistance Army (LRA) assailants attacked the village, killing 12 civilians, kidnapping more than 100 others (including children) and setting fire to and looting the village.

- On July 22, in Oslo, Norway, a politically-motivated lone wolf first detonated a VBIED outside the Prime Minister's office, killing seven government employees and one civilian and wounding 30 other civilians. Two hours later, on Utoya Island, the same assailant then fired upon a Norwegian Labor Party-associated youth camp, killing 67 people and two police officers and injuring 66 others.

(1,528 words)

Unit 3

Global Financial Crimes

Part Ⅰ In-class Reading

Pre-reading Questions

- *Please discuss with your partners about the relationship between the financing the terrorists get and the acts the terrorists conduct.*
- *Have you ever heard of any informal value transfer system before? What role do you think those systems play in the terrorist organizations?*
- *Based on your knowledge, could you give suitable solutions to deal with financing terror?*

Text A

Financing Terror

The frequency and seriousness of international terrorist acts are often proportionate to the financing that terrorist groups might get. Terrorist organizations must develop and maintain robust and low-key funding sources to survive. Domestic and international terrorist groups raise money in the United States to exploit the nation's market-based economy and democratic freedoms for profits that they send overseas or use locally to finance sleeper cells. Raising funds on American soil fulfills complementary goals by undermining the economy, introducing counterfeit and often unsafe or adulterated products and pharmaceuticals into the consumer market, and increasing the social costs of substance abuse by feeding the demand for illicit drugs.

The terrorists who attacked the World Trade Center in New York City in 1993 originally planned to use a larger bomb to bring down both towers by toppling one into the other. They also wanted to amplify the carnage by augmenting their vehicle-borne improvised explosive device with a chemical or biological weapon to increase casualties and hamper rescue efforts. Their goal, however, went awry because they ran out of money.

Similarly, lack of funds limited the plans of another group that conspired in 2003 to simultaneously bomb the Egyptian, American, and other Western embassies in Pakistan. Inadequate monetary resources forced the group to focus on attacking only the Egyptian embassy. "A short time before the bombing of the [Egyptian] embassy the assigned group... told us that they could strike both the Egyptian and American embassies if we gave them enough money. We had already provided them with all that we had and we couldn't collect more money."

A major source of terrorist funding involves criminal activities. Groups use a wide variety of low-risk, high-reward crimes to finance their operations.

Those most likely encountered by local law enforcement involve six primary areas.

Illicit Drugs

"If we cannot kill them with guns, so we will kill them with drugs." Documented links exist between terrorist groups and drug trafficking, notably the smuggling of pseudoephedrine, a precursor used to manufacture methamphetamine. After purchasing the substance in multi-ton quantities, smugglers associated with one terrorist group moved truckloads of it into the

United States to feed methamphetamine labs in California and neighboring southwestern states.

In three major drug investigations, DEA arrested more than 300 people and seized over $16 million in currency and enough pseudoephedrine to manufacture 370,000 pounds of methamphetamine. To put this quantity into context, the average annual seizure of methamphetamine throughout the United States in 2002 was 6,000 pounds.

Fraud

Frauds perpetrated by terrorist groups include identity theft for profit and credit card, welfare, social security, insurance, food stamp, and coupon fraud. Industry experts estimate that $3.5 billion in coupons are redeemed annually. About 10 percent, or $3.5 million, is fraudulent.

In 1987, authorities disrupted a large coupon fraud ring involving more than 70 participants. The conspirators were accused of sending a portion of the proceeds to Palestine Liberation Organization (PLO) bank accounts in the Middle East and Europe. A Palestinian operating several grocery stores in the North Miami area, Florida, was the key player in a nationwide money laundering and financing operation for the PLO. The investigation discovered that 72 individuals from throughout the United States gathered in Hollywood, Florida, to further the fraudulent coupon distribution network. One person was identified as a cell leader of a terrorist network. Members of the group also were involved in hijacking trucks and selling stolen food stamps and property.

In 1994, New York City officials identified the head of a coupon fraud ring who had established a network of stores by targeting those owned and controlled by Middle Eastern businessmen willing to participate in schemes that defrauded American commercial enterprises. Most of the time, a small store that normally submitted $200 to $300 in coupons monthly would suddenly begin sending in tens of thousands of dollars worth of them after joining the network. The store owners never saw the coupons; they only received the redemption checks. In many cases, the owners borrowed money or agreed to lease stores for a monthly fee set by the network. They used coupons to pay the debt on these loans, which sometimes required 49 percent interest per month.

Stolen Baby Formula

In another scheme in the late 1990s, investigators in Texas discovered that organized shoplifting gangs paid drug addicts and indigent people $1 per can to steal baby formula. The groups repackaged the products in counterfeit cardboard boxes before shipping the bootleg formula to unsuspecting stores across the United States. One of the largest rings at the time netted $44 million in 18 months. As the terrorist attacks on September 11 unfolded, a Texas state trooper pulled over a rental van and found an enormous load of infant formula inside. Police later identified the driver as a member of a terrorist group and linked him to a nationwide theft ring that specialized in reselling stolen infant formula and wiring the proceeds to the Middle East. The investigation led to felony charges against more than 40 suspects, about half of them illegal immigrants. Police also seized $2.7 million in stolen assets, including $1 million worth of formula. This investigation was only the beginning. In the years after September 11, police discovered and disrupted several regional and national theft rings specializing in shoplifted baby formula. At least eight of the major cases involved individuals of Middle Eastern descent or who had ties to that region.

Intellectual Property Theft

According to media reports, the terrorists who bombed the World Trade Center in 1993 allegedly financed their activities with counterfeit textile sales from a store in New York City. A raid on a souvenir shop led to the seizure of a suitcase full of counterfeit watches and the discovery of flight manuals for Boeing 767s, some containing handwritten notes in Arabic. A subsequent raid on a counterfeit handbag shop yielded faxes relating to the purchase of bridge inspection equipment. While investigating an assault on a member of an organized crime syndicate two weeks later, police found fake driver's licenses and lists of suspected terrorists, including the names of some workers from the handbag shop, in the man's apartment.

Pirated software constitutes a tremendous source of funds for transnational criminal syndicates, as well as terrorist groups. It is not difficult to see why software piracy has become attractive. A drug dealer would pay about $47,000 for a kilo of cocaine and then sell it on the street for approximately $94,000, reaping a 100 percent profit. But, for the same outlay of $47,000 and substantially less risk, an intellectual property thief could buy 1,500 bootleg copies of a popular software program and resell them for a profit of 900 percent. To put these numbers into context, the September 11 attacks cost approximately $500,000, or $26,000 per terrorist. One successful large-scale intellectual property crime easily could fund multiple terrorist attacks on the scale of those of September 11, 2001.

Cigarette Smuggling

Exploiting a considerable tax differential, smugglers bought van loads of cigarettes for cash in North Carolina and transported them to Michigan. According to prosecutors, each trip netted $3,000 to $10,000. In one year, the recipient of the profits, who had links to a terrorist group, had deposited over $735,000 in bank accounts while paying for houses, luxury cars, and other goods with cash. The group sent items, such as night-vision goggles, cameras and scopes, surveying equipment, global positioning systems, and mine and metal detection equipment, to other terrorists abroad. The ringleader was sentenced to 155 years in prison, and his second in command received a 70-year prison sentence.

Informal Value Transfer Systems

Informal value transfer and alternative remittance systems play a significant role in terrorism financing. One example, hawala, involves the transfer or remittance of money from one party to another, normally without the use of such formal financial institutions as banks or money exchanges. International financial institutions estimate annual hawala transfers at approximately two trillion dollars, representing two percent of international financial transactions.

Because these systems operate below legal and financial radars, they are susceptible to abuse by criminal elements and terrorists. Moreover, few elements of this informal transfer system are recorded, making it difficult to obtain records of the transmitters and the beneficiaries or to capture the scale and magnitude of such transfers. Although operators keep ledgers, their records often are written in idiosyncratic shorthand and maintained only briefly.

Conclusion

From stolen baby formula to intellectual property theft, terrorist groups employ a variety of criminal schemes to raise funds. And, as with other homeland security matters, countering terrorist financing is fundamentally a local law enforcement responsibility. The more familiar officers are with the criminal enterprises used by these groups to raise money, the more effective they will be in finding ways to counter such activities.

Countermeasures must disrupt terrorist financing and starve such groups of the money necessary to sustain their organizations and to perpetrate attacks. Without the financial means to carry out their missions, terrorists will find it increasingly difficult to continue their wanton acts of death and destruction.

(1,503 words)

Background Information

▶ DEA

The Drug Enforcement Administration (DEA) was created by President Richard Nixon through an Executive Order in July 1973 in order to establish a single unified command to combat "an all-out global war on the drug menace". At its outset, DEA had 1,470 Special Agents and a budget of less than $75 million. Today, the DEA has nearly 5,000 Special Agents and a budget of $2.02 billion.

DEA is a United States federal law enforcement agency under the U.S. Department of Justice, tasked with combating drug smuggling and use within the United States. Not only is the DEA the lead agency for domestic enforcement of the Controlled Substances Act, sharing concurrent jurisdiction with the Federal Bureau of Investigation (FBI) and Immigration and Customs Enforcement (ICE), it also has sole responsibility for coordinating and pursuing U.S. drug investigations abroad. The DEA is headed by an Administrator of Drug Enforcement appointed by the President of the United States and confirmed by the U.S. Senate.

▶ food stamp

The Supplemental Nutrition Assistance Program (SNAP), formerly known as the Food Stamp Program, provides food-purchasing assistance for low-and no-income people living in the U.S. SNAP is the largest nutrition assistance program. It is a federal aid program, administered by the U.S. Department of Agriculture, under the Food and Nutrition Service (FNS), though benefits are distributed by each U.S. state's Division of Social Services or Children and Family Services.

▶ Hawala

Hawala (used interchangeably with Hundi) is an alternative or parallel remittance system. It exists and operates parallel to the "traditional" banking channels. The components of Hawala that distinguish it from other remittance systems are trust and extensive use of connections such as family relationships or regional affiliations. Transfers of money take place based on communications between members of a network of Hawaladars, or Hawala dealers. It works by transferring money without actually moving it. In fact "money transfer without money movement" is a well-recognized definition of Hawala. The system is based on trust-cash in and cash out, but no physical movement takes place. The transaction takes one or two days and is faster than most bank wire transfers, without requiring opening of accounts. The whole transaction is consummated without leaving a paper trail.

The Hawala/Hundi or so called "underground banking" have often been associated with ethnic groups from Africa and Asia, and commonly involve the transfer of value between countries, but outside the legitimate banking system. The system has emanated from lack of effective anti-money laundering programs, laws or regulations, coupled with legal systems that do not encourage information sharing and law enforcement cooperation.

To go into the historical perspective of Hawala, it was born centuries before the Western financial systems, in Indian and Chinese civilizations to facilitate the secure movement of funds to China and India. Merchant traders wishing to send funds to their homelands would deposit them with a Hawala "banker", who normally owned a trading business. For a small fee the banker would arrange for the funds to be available for withdrawal from another "banker", normally also a trader, in another country. The two bankers would settle accounts through the normal process of trade.

Today, the process works much the same, with people in various parts of the world using their corporate accounts to move money internationally for third parties. In this manner the deposits and withdrawals are made through Hawala bankers, rather than through traditional financial institutions.

New Words

proportionate [prəˈpɔːʃənɪt]

adj. Proportionate means the same as. (与……)成比例的

E.g. The head of the Association of Chief Police Officers has insisted the policing of demonstrations in the UK is "proportionate" and that recent criticisms lack objectivity and perspective.

domestic [dəˈmɛstɪk]

adj. 1) Domestic political activities, events, and situations happen or exist within one particular country. 国内的

E.g. "There is a huge demand for domestic plastics and no supply," said spokeswoman Niki Audsley.

2) Domestic duties and activities are concerned with the running of a home and family. 家务的

E.g. …a plan for sharing domestic chores.

3) Domestic items and services are intended to be used in people's homes rather than in factories or offices. 家用的

E.g. …domestic appliances.

4) A domestic situation or atmosphere is one which involves a family and their home. 家庭的

E.g. It was a scene of such domestic bliss.

5) A domestic animal is one that is not wild and is kept either on a farm to produce food or in someone's home as a pet. 家养的;饲养的

E.g. … a domestic cat.

complementary [ˌkɒmplɪˈmɛntərɪ, -ˈmɛntrɪ]

adj. 1) Complementary things are different from each other but make a good combination. 互补的

E.g. The company also said the two businesses were complementary because they used different investment strategies.

2) Complementary medicine refers to ways of treating patients which are different from the ones used by most Western doctors, for example acupuncture and homeopathy. 辅助性的

E.g. Despite the high price, the impact might be temporary without the addition of complementary treatments.

counterfeit [ˈkaʊntəfɪt]

adj. Counterfeit money, goods, or documents are not genuine, but have been made to look exactly like genuine ones in order to deceive people. 伪造的

E.g. He admitted possessing and delivering counterfeit currency.

[C] *n.* 仿制品;伪造品

E.g. Some violate U.S. laws by selling counterfeit or expired medicines or dispensing without a valid doctor's prescription.

vt. If someone counterfeits something, they make a version of it that is not genuine but has been made to look genuine in order to deceive people. 仿冒;伪造

adulterate [əˈdʌltəreɪt]

vt. If something such as food or drink is adulterated, someone has made its quality worse by adding water or cheaper products to it. (给食物、饮料等)掺假

E.g. It was reported that the food had been adulterated for many years.

pharmaceutical [ˌfɑːməˈsjuːtɪkəl]

adj. Pharmaceutical means connected with the industrial production of medicines. 制药的

E.g. They reviewed 30 studies analysing research projects, which had been funded by a pharmaceutical company.

n. (*pl.*) Pharmaceuticals are medicines. 药品

E.g. Antibiotics were of no use, neither were other pharmaceuticals.

topple [ˈtɒpəl]

vt. /*vi.* If someone or something topples somewhere or if you topple them, they become unsteady or unstable and fall over. 倒下

E.g. He just released his hold and toppled slowly backwards.

vt. To topple a government or leader, especially one that is not elected by the people, means to cause them to lose power. [新闻]推翻

E.g. The premier also needs to prevent another big bank collapse, since that could topple his government.

amplify [ˈæmplɪˌfaɪ]

vt. 1) If you amplify a sound, you make it louder, usually by using electronic equipment. 扩大(声音)

E.g. The music was amplified with microphones.

2) To amplify something means to increase its strength or intensity. 增强

E.g. American journalists can, and should, amplify the voices of those who are unheard.

carnage [ˈkɑːnɪdʒ]

[U] *n.* Carnage is the violent killing of large numbers of people, especially in a war. 大屠杀

E.g. The full horror of the carnage caused by the bomb is revealed in the programme.

augment [ɔːgˈmɛnt]

vt. To augment something means to make it larger, stronger, or more effective by adding something to it. [正式]增加

E.g. The new agreement will augment existing free trade agreements among the four countries.

hamper [ˈhæmpə]

vt. If someone or something hampers you, they make it difficult for you to do what you are trying to do. 妨碍

E.g. The bad weather hampered rescue operations.

恶劣的天气阻碍了救助行动。

conspire [kən'spaɪə]

vi. If two or more people or groups conspire to do something illegal or harmful, they make a secret agreement to do it. 合谋

E.g. They deny conspiring together to smuggle drugs.

vt. /*vi.* If events conspire to produce a particular result, they seem to work together to cause this result. 协同

E.g. Everything conspired to make her life a misery.

pseudoephedrine [ˌsjuːdəʊ'ɛfɪˌdriːn, -ˌdrɪn]

[U] *n.* a drug similar in action to ephedrine, used extensively as a decongestant 假麻黄碱

precursor [prɪ'kɜːsə]

[C] *n.* ~ (of/to sth.) (formal) a person or a thing that comes before sb./sth. similar and that leads to or influences its development 先驱,前导

E.g. He said that the deal should not be seen as a precursor to a merger.

methamphetamine [ˌmɛθæm'fɛtəmɪn]

[U] *n.* a variety of amphetamine used for its stimulant action 甲基苯丙胺

perpetrate ['pɜːpɪˌtreɪt]

vt. If someone perpetrates a crime or any other immoral or harmful act, they do it. 犯(罪);做(不道德、有害之事)

E.g. A high proportion of crime in any country is perpetrated by young males in their teens and twenties.

hijack ['haɪˌdʒæk]

vt. If someone hijacks a plane or other vehicle, they illegally take control of it by force while it is travelling from one place to another. 劫持

E.g. It is difficult to tell exactly whether the same group is hijacking these ships.

→派生词 hijacking [C] *n.* 劫持

E.g. The Taliban had given safe haven to al-Qaeda, which had carried out the hijacking of four airliners to attack New York and Washington, in which more than 3,000 people died.

defraud [dɪˈfrɔːd]

vt. If someone defrauds you, they take something away from you or stop you from getting what belongs to you by means of tricks and lies. 骗取

E.g. Five people have been charged in connection with attempting to defraud an online bank.

redemption [rɪˈdɛmpʃən]

[U] *n.* Redemption is the act of redeeming something or of being redeemed by something. 救赎;偿还

E.g. He craves redemption for his sins.

felony [ˈfɛlənɪ]

[C] *n.* In countries where the legal system distinguishes between very serious crimes and less serious ones, a felony is a very serious crime such as armed robbery. [法]重罪

E.g. He pleaded guilty to those felonies.

raid [reɪd]

vt. When soldiers raid a place, they make a sudden armed attack against it, with the aim of causing damage rather than occupying any of the enemy's land. 突袭

E.g. Sudan Armed Forces spokesman Sawarmi Khaled Saad vehemently denied any links to the raid.

[C] *n.* 突袭

vt. If the police raid a building, they enter it suddenly and by force in order to look for dangerous criminals or for evidence of something illegal, such as drugs or weapons. 突击搜查

E.g. Police raided their headquarters and other offices.

[C] *n.* 突击搜查

E.g. Once again FBI were on the scene when local police officers carried out the raid.

syndicate [ˈsɪndɪkeɪt]

[C] *n.* a group of people or companies who work together and help each other in order to achieve a particular aim 联合组织,财团

E.g. Chief Superintendent John Ribeiro of the Narcotics Bureau said police acted after receiving a tip-off about a South American transnational drug syndicate.

vt. When newspaper articles or television programmes are syndicated, they are sold to several different newspapers or television stations, who then publish the articles or broadcast the programmes. (将稿子或电视节目)出售给多个媒体

E.g. Today his programme is syndicated to 500 stations.

prosecutor [ˈprɒsɪˌkjuːtə]

[C] *n.* In some countries, a prosecutor is a lawyer or official who brings charges against someone or tries to prove in a trial that they are guilty. 起诉人;检察官

E.g. The officers found heroin when they searched his car with O'Neal's consent, the prosecutor said.

sentence [ˈsɛntəns]

[C] *n.* In a law court, a sentence is the punishment that a person receives after they have been found guilty of a crime. 刑罚

E.g. He was given a ten-year sentence.

vt. When a judge sentences someone, he or she states in court what their punishment will be. 宣判;判决

E.g. The criminal was sentenced to eight years in prison.

remittance [rɪˈmɪtəns]

[C] *n.* A remittance is a sum of money that you send to someone. 汇款

E.g. Remittance can be made by cheque or credit card.

ledger [ˈlɛdʒə]

[C] *n.* A ledger is a book in which a company or organization writes down the amounts of money it spends and receives. [商]分类账

idiosyncratic [ˌɪdɪəʊsɪŋˈkrætɪk]

adj. If you describe someone's actions or characteristics as idiosyncratic, you mean that they are somewhat unusual. 怪异的;另类的

E.g. Dr Janda said it suggested that people's behaviour may be idiosyncratic, rather than reasoned and predictable.

wanton [ˈwɒntən]

adj. A wanton action deliberately causes harm, damage, or waste without having any reason to. 有意伤害的

E.g. But for the people who lived here, this is a story of wanton destruction.

Exercises

▶ Exercise One: Reading comprehension

Answer the following questions in your own words after reading the passage.

1. What message can you get from the two terrorist attacks happening to the World Trade Center in New York City in 1993 and the Egyptian embassy in 2003?
2. What criminal activities do frauds perpetrated by terrorist groups include?
3. What was the key player in a nationwide money laundering and financing operation for the Palestine Liberation Organization (PLO)?
4. Why is intellectual property crime, compared with drug trafficking, more attractive for transnational criminal syndicates, as well as terrorist groups?
5. Why do informal value transfer and alternative remittance systems play a significant role in terrorism financing?

▶ Exercise Two: Translation

Please translate the following sentences into Chinese.

1. The frequency and seriousness of international terrorist acts are often proportionate

to the financing that terrorist groups might get.

2. Raising funds on American soil fulfills complementary goals by undermining the economy, introducing counterfeit and often unsafe or adulterated products and pharmaceuticals into the consumer market, and increasing the social costs of substance abuse by feeding the demand for illicit drugs.
3. In 1994, New York City officials identified the head of a coupon fraud ring who had established a network of stores by targeting those owned and controlled by Middle Eastern businessmen willing to participate in schemes that defrauded American commercial enterprises.
4. Because these systems operate below legal and financial radars, they are susceptible to abuse by criminal elements and terrorists. Moreover, few elements of this informal transfer system are recorded, making it difficult to obtain records of the transmitters and the beneficiaries or to capture the scale and magnitude of such transfers.

Part II After-class Reading

Text B

Dealing with Hawala

—*Informal Financial Centers in the Ethnic Community*

Today, hawala constitutes an important economic aspect of life in America's Middle Eastern and Southeast Asian communities. Law enforcement officers who work in these locations or investigate white-collar crime or terrorism financing should know about and understand how to deal with hawala and other nontraditional financial centers.

How Hawala Works

Hawala comprises one type of the informal value transfer system (IVTS) used mostly by members of an ethnic community to send money around the world. Other forms of IVTS, which also can be elements of hawala, include physically transporting (smuggling) currency and stored-value transfers (chits). Hawala does not involve the immediate movement of any negotiable instrument nor are actual funds immediately transmitted anywhere. An ancient system that actually predates banking, it works in an analogous manner to a more formal system of "wiring" money. When individuals wire money, they contact a legitimate money-wiring service and provide an amount of funds they wish to send to another party plus a fee. If they send money overseas, they generally pay a recognized margin or exchange rate at which they purchase funds in that country's currency. Of course, funds are not actually "wired" to the other person, and nobody physically sends money anywhere at that time. Instead, one vendor accepts the cash from the sender, and another gives the same amount to the recipient. Then, the two vendors settle at a later time.

In more legitimate operations, these settling transactions almost always involve the transfer of funds from one account to another at banking institutions. With hawala, however, either a transfer of funds to a bank or a number of less formal settling transactions may occur. Hawaladars (i.e., operators) may travel overseas on a regular basis to settle accounts in person with their contacts. They may have other business interests with these intermediaries that involve inventory and merchandise, which they can manipulate to reflect the hawala transactions. For example, hawaladars can trade premium goods, such as phone cards, at a discount to represent the value of earlier transactions.

Just like legitimate money-wiring operations, hawala often is contained within another community business, such as an ethnic market or travel agency, or run by freelancers who operate autonomously in the community. The global scope of IVTS and hawala is impossible to calculate. An International Monetary Fund/World Bank estimate puts worldwide IVTS transfers on the order of tens of billions of dollars annually.

Money Laundering

Hawala is not necessarily synonymous with money laundering or even white-collar crime or terrorism financing. Money laundering, by its very nature, involves attempting to make "dirty" money, often via drug activity or organized crime wherein criminals generate sums of wealth (usually cash) that cannot be easily explained or managed, "clean". So, they transfer the money in and out of different accounts, banks, and various legitimate and partially legitimate businesses. This supposedly creates ambiguity as to its origin and lends legitimacy to otherwise criminal proceeds. It is significant to recall that money laundering, per se, generally is not, in and of itself, a criminal act. Most money-laundering statutes require evidence of a specific underlying enterprise, such as drug trafficking or other criminal activity, to successfully prosecute the money-laundering offense.

Terrorism Financing

An interesting paradox surrounds the financing of terrorism. First, cash proves as important, if not more so, to successful terrorist operations as it does to any other prosperous venture, legal or otherwise. But, at the opposite end of the equation, terrorist operations are not prohibitively expensive. After all, a teenage terrorist who straps on explosives and detonates himself in a Tel Aviv restaurant killing dozens costs little, yet his actions prove effective.

Ahmed Ressam, an Algerian loosely affiliated with al-Qaeda, had lived illegally in Canada for several years when he tried to enter the United States with explosives in the trunk of his car. He was destined for Los Angeles International Airport where he intended to set off an explosion as part of a larger New Year's millennium terrorism plot. His overseas handlers had instructed him to finance himself by burglarizing hotel rooms, stealing credit cards, and committing other petty offenses. Timothy McVeigh and Terry Nichols used the proceeds from several home burglaries and gun show sales to buy farm-grade fertilizer they mixed with fuel oil to bomb the Murrah Federal Building in Oklahoma City.

According to the 9/11 Commission, the entire cost of the September 11 plot was between \$400,000 and \$500,000. Considering that close to two dozen individuals (the 19 hijackers plus overseas support elements) were likely involved over an 18-month to 2-year period, the funds needed for significant international travel, terrorist-camp training, flight school, and living expenses only approximated \$12,000 per person, per year.

The 9/11 Commission also found no evidence of any foreign government knowingly helping to finance the operation; instead, most of the funds were derived from donations to charity. While some media sources have claimed Saudi Arabia was responsible for providing a large amount of terrorism funding in general and particularly for the September 11 plot, a specific dollar-for-dollar nexus does not exist. While the royal family in Saudi Arabia maintains a complex relationship with both its citizens and conservative religious clerics and charities in the country, proving the government provided funds to these religious leaders and charities knowing that the money would eventually finance terrorism never has been established. Moreover, while the 9/11 Commission found that al-Qaeda used hawala to move money in and out of Afghanistan, it also determined that the group did not employ hawala in any way to fund the 19 hijackers or the events surrounding the September 11 attacks.

Hawala in the Community

People use hawala for any number of reasons; many of these are legitimate, while others are not. Investigators must understand that in the

Middle Eastern community, the importance of family and other trusted relationships cannot be overemphasized. Often, a member of the community refers to another as belonging to a particular family when, in fact, the relationship is so distant that it is legally insignificant. These family and clan relationships perhaps are more significant than in any other ethnic community in the United States. At the same time, many members have relatives in their home countries they support financially.

Within these Middle Eastern and Southeast Asian communities, members trust local businessmen, including the hawaladar, a great deal. That trust is one element that invites the use of hawala. A fictional example of a member of the community employed in violation of his tourist or student visa can help illustrate the system. The young man does not have a social security number and wishes to send money to his homeland, a country where currently it is unlawful to do so, to support relatives. He has four immediate incentives to use a local hawaladar, rather than a traditional bank or money-wiring service.

1) He is violating the terms of his visa by working in the United States.

2) He does not have a social security number and may be working without paying taxes.

3) Treasury regulations do not allow him to legally send money to his country.

4) A hawaladar probably is more economical than other more legitimate means of moving money because of lower finance charges and exchange rates.

Passed in 2001, the United and Strengthening of America by Providing Appropriate Tools Required to Intercept and Obstruct Terrorism (USA PATRIOT) Act called on the U.S. Department of the Treasury to determine whether Congress should stiffen laws relating to IVTS in the United States. The report to Congress concluded that "although law enforcement chases the informal remittance providers further 'underground', outlawing the activity also deprives the mostly law-abiding IVTS customers of the primary channel through which they transfer funds."

Techniques for Law Enforcement

As with any crime problem, a keen understanding of who is who in the community constitutes one of the keys to successfully dealing with hawala. Officers and investigators need to use their sources of information to determine which merchants and individuals in the community act as IVTS brokers. When suspicion arises that these entities are employing IVTS to facilitate drug trafficking, terrorism financing, or money laundering, law enforcement can exploit a host of local, state, and federal offenses these enterprises are committing.

Regardless of how well-meaning or "community oriented" hawaladars are, they violate technical infractions each time they engage in a financial transaction. The federal Bank Secrecy Act (BSA) requires any person or group acting as a money-services business (MSB) to adhere to numerous reporting and record-keeping requirements, most or all of which hawaladars routinely ignore.

Additionally, these businesses, by law, must register with the Department of the Treasury's Financial Crimes Enforcement Network (FinCEN), which, again, they usually disregard. Furthermore, MSBs are required by law to produce suspicious activity reports (SARs) for transactions over $2,000 that appear, or should appear to them, to involve illegal activity. Finally (although not all-inclusively), investigators should note that Title 18 of the U.S. Code makes it a crime to operate an MSB in the absence of compliance with applicable state licensing requirements. Undoubtedly, these enterprises also do not appropriately follow these regulations.

A misperception exists that hawaladars do not keep records; this is false.

Many keep extensive documentation because the settling of accounts often takes place well into the future. What investigators need to look for are unconventional records or ones kept in a language other than English. Also, because hawaladars barter in other than cash products, investigators should check for large transactions involving food stamps, lottery tickets, and phone cards, all of which can be alternate forms of currency in the community. Of course, phone records and those from Internet service providers, as well as legitimate bank documents, can be valuable because they show who the hawaladar has dealt with. Investigators should focus on contacts and transactions that involve Great Britain, Switzerland, and Dubai as these comprise major financial centers with strict financial secrecy laws. Moreover, even when hawaladars are not knowingly involved in serious illegal activity, their nonconforming business practices put them in positions where they could assist law enforcement with the real criminal element in a community, especially those dealing in narcotics, laundering money, or financing terrorism.

Conclusion

The hawala concept is not prohibitively complicated. Its deviance from conventional banking and financial institutions, together with its place in the Middle Eastern and Southeast Asian communities, can pose a challenge for investigators experienced in more traditional financial crimes, including money laundering and terrorism financing. However, employing some specific techniques, coupled with a solid community intelligence base, should assist them with hawala and nontraditional financial centers.

(1,759 words)

Unit 4

Drug Trafficking

Part Ⅰ In-class Reading

Pre-reading Questions

- *Have you ever got to know any information of drug trafficking before? Can you share anything you know with your classmates?*
- *Can you figure out the relationship between drug trafficking and money laundering?*
- *Why is international police cooperation crucial to tackling drug trafficking?*

Text A

Dismantling Transnational Drug Networks

Key U.S. foreign policy tools available for targeting major drug traffickers and their illicit networks include establishing extradition agreements with foreign countries, freezing and blocking foreign criminal assets within U.S. jurisdiction, and building foreign capacity to investigate, arrest, prosecute, and incarcerate drug traffickers domestically.

Extradition to the United States

The U.S. government regularly uses extradition as an important judicial tool against suspected drug traffickers located abroad. Extradition refers to the formal surrender of a person by a state to another state for prosecution. Proponents of extradition to the United States argue that suspected criminals are more likely to receive a fair trial in U.S. courts than in countries where the local judicial process may be corrupt and where suspects can use bribes and intimidation to manipulate the outcome of a trial.

U.S. bilateral judicial cooperation with Mexico and Colombia is often cited as particularly exemplary, yielding record numbers of extradited traffickers to the United States. Colombia, for example, has extradited more than 1,400 individuals to the United States since December 17, 1997. In 2012, Mexico extradited 115 individuals to the United States, including 52 for narcotics-related offenses.

Some anecdotal evidence appears to suggest that the threat of extradition has affected the behavior of foreign drug trafficking organizations. For example, some Colombian drug traffickers are reportedly distancing themselves from overt drug distribution activities, which could be used as evidence to trigger extradition. Nevertheless, this counterdrug tool remains controversial and is not universally supported. Afghanistan, for example, does not have a formal extradition or mutual legal assistance arrangement with the United States. Many countries simply refuse to extradite drug traffickers, citing concerns about the potential use of the death penalty in the United States against its citizens and state sovereignty rights. Burma is one such country, which continues to refuse to extradite four suspected drug traffickers under indictment in the United States. Some observers claim that suspected traffickers often take advantage of such limitations in the extradition system and seek safe haven in countries that are unwilling to extradite.

Targeting Illicit Drug Profits

To reap the financial benefits of the illegal drug trade, traffickers must launder their illicit profits into the licit economy. As a result, the United States and other members of the international community have sought to use anti-money laundering efforts as a tool to combat this upstream activity in the illegal drug market. Currently, several U.S. agencies are involved in international anti-money laundering efforts designed to enhance financial transaction transparency and regulation, improve cooperation and coordination with foreign governments and private financial institutions, and provide foreign countries with law enforcement training and support.

Congress has been active in pursuing anti-money laundering regulations and program oversight. In 1999, Congress passed the Foreign Narcotics Kingpin Designation Act to authorize the President to target the financial profits that significant foreign narcotics traffickers and their organizations (known as "Specially Designated Narcotics Trafficker Kingpins", or SDNTKs) have accumulated from their illicit activities. This tool seeks to deny SDNTKs and their related businesses access to the U.S. financial system and all trade transactions involving U.S. companies and individuals.

Following the September 11, 2001 terrorist attacks, Congress further strengthened U.S. measures to combat money laundering by providing the Secretary of the Treasury with new authorities to impose a set of regulatory restrictions, or "special measures", against foreign jurisdictions, foreign financial institutions, and certain classes of financial transactions involving foreign jurisdictions, if deemed by the Treasury Secretary to be "of primary money laundering concern". These anti-money laundering tools are designed not only to address drug trafficking, but also to combat other forms of related criminal activity, including terrorist financing.

In addition, Congress requires that the State Department include in its annual International Narcotics Control Strategy Report (INCSR) a separate volume devoted to the state of international money laundering and financial crimes in each country. Among the report's congressionally mandated requirements, the State Department annually identifies the world's "major money laundering countries," defined as those countries "whose financial institutions engage in currency transactions involving significant amounts of proceeds from international narcotics trafficking" and other serious crimes.

Other agencies involved in targeting drug trafficking-related financial assets include the Department of Justice, through its asset forfeiture activities, and the Department of Homeland Security's Immigration Customs and Enforcement agency, which developed an Illicit Pathways Attack Strategy (IPAS) to target illicit financial activity of transnational organized crime networks operating in the Western Hemisphere.

U.S. officials and some observers have highlighted the value of anti-money laundering efforts in combating drug trafficking. In 2007, the Treasury Department's Office of Foreign Assets Control (OFAC) reported that anti-money laundering efforts against Colombian drug cartels have been effective in isolating and incapacitating designated supporters, businesses, and front companies linked to the Cali Cartel and Norte del Valle Cartel. Some observers also describe the Treasury Secretary's additional authorities to designate jurisdictions of primary money laundering concern and apply "special measures" against these jurisdictions as having "potentially profound effects successfully resulted in the freezing of some $25 million in North Korean assets—funds that reportedly included counterfeit U.S. currency and profits from other North Korean criminal activity, including drug trafficking.

Skeptics of the use of anti-money laundering efforts to combat drug trafficking argue that tracking illicit financial transactions may be more difficult and may yield less success than other counterdrug tools. The same types of money laundering methods—bulk cash smuggling, tradebased money laundering, and others—that the State Department identified as issues of concern more than a decade ago remain among the most used forms of money laundering today. Further, emerging challenges include the growing volume of financial transactions, especially the volume of international electronic transfers, and the movement of illegal money laundering outside formal banking channels, including through "hawala"-type chains of transnational money brokers and through the use of stored-value cards.

Building Foreign Law Enforcement and Prosecution Capacity

Another element of U.S. efforts to dismantle foreign drug networks involves providing foreign countries with the tools which improve their domestic efforts to dismantle drug networks. Such assistance, in the form of training, equipping, and other institutional capacity building, ultimately seeks to strengthen foreign judicial and law enforcement institutions and assist in developing host nation administrative infrastructures to combat the illicit drug trade. Institutional development programs focus mainly on fighting corruption and training to support criminal justice system reforms and the rule of law. A variety of U.S. agencies are involved in counterdrug-related capacity building efforts abroad, including the State Department, USAID, the Department of Justice, Department of Homeland Security, and the Department of Defense.

For example, the State Department funds a series of International Law Enforcement Academies (ILEAs) and Regional Training Centers (RTCs) that provide training and technical assistance to foreign law enforcement practitioners on a variety of subjects, including counternarcotics. ILEAs are located in Gabarone, Botswana; Bangkok, Thailand; Budapest, Hungary; Rosewell, NM; and San Salvador, El Salvador. RTCs are located in Lima, Peru; and Accra, Ghana.

Several U.S. agencies also provide foreign law enforcement training and assistance in order to enhance interdiction efforts abroad. The Department of

State, the U.S. Coast Guard, U.S. Customs and Border Protection, the DEA, and the FBI are involved in providing anti-narcotics law enforcement training, technical assistance, and equipment for foreign personnel. For example, the DEA, through its Sensitive Investigative Units overseas, sponsors a range of capacity and coordination projects in countries such as Afghanistan, Colombia, the Dominican Republic, Honduras, Ecuador, Guatemala, Mexico, Nigeria, Panama, Paraguay, Peru, Ghana, and Thailand. Other efforts include the FBI's National Gang Task Force and the State Department's Central American Law Enforcement Exchange program. The U.S. military provides international support for drug monitoring and detection. In addition, the United States regularly contributes funding and expertise to law enforcement assistance activities of the United Nations and other international organizations.

According to the State Department, drug trafficking organizations often seek to subvert or corrupt governments in order to guarantee a secure operating environment and essentially "buy their way into power". Anti-corruption efforts thus seek to prevent traffickers from undermining the legitimacy and effectiveness of foreign government institutions. Some observers, however, argue that counterdrug policies are placing too little emphasis on projects that help foreign countries develop a culture supportive of the rule of law. One expert explained in congressional testimony in 2007, "unless foreign police organizations recognize and internalize what the rule of law means, what its key characteristics are, and why the rule of law is necessary to accomplish their mission, no amount of aid will get the job done."

(1,414 words)

Background Information

▶ The Cali Cartel

The Cali Cartel was a drug cartel based in southern Colombia, around the city of Cali and the Valle del Cauca Department. The Cali Cartel, whose brief roots began in trafficking marijuana, soon shifted to cocaine due to its ease of transporting and greater profit margin. Cali would be the dominant group in trafficking South American heroin due to their access to the opium growing areas of Colombia. At the height of the Cali Cartel's reign, they were cited as having control over 90% of the world's cocaine market and for being directly responsible for the growth of the cocaine market in Europe, controlling 90% of the market.

▶ Norte del Valle Cartel

The Norte del Valle Cartel, or North Valley Cartel, was a drug cartel that operated principally in the north of the Valle del Cauca department of Colombia. It rose to prominence during the second half of the 1990s, after the Cali Cartel and the Medellín Cartel fragmented, and it was known as one of the most powerful organizations in the illegal drugs trade. The drug cartel was led by the brothers Luis Enrique and Javier Antonio Calle Serna, alias "Los Comba", until its delivery in 2012 to the authorities of the United States.

▶ Bulk cash smuggling

Bulk Cash Smuggling is a reporting offense under the Bank Secrecy Act, and is part of the United States Code (U.S.C.). The code stipulates: Whoever, with the intent to evade a currency reporting requirement, knowingly conceals more than $10,000 in currency or other monetary instruments on the person of such individual or in any conveyance, article of luggage, merchandise, or other container, and transports or transfers or attempts to transport or transfer such currency or monetary instruments from a place within the United States to a place outside of the United

States, or from a place outside the United States to a place within the United States, shall be guilty of a currency smuggling offense.

▶ Tradebased money laundering

Tradebased money laundering is an alternative remittance system that allows illegal organizations the opportunity to earn, move and store proceeds disguised as legitimate trade. Value can be moved through this process by false-invoicing, over-invoicing and under-invoicing commodities that are imported or exported around the world.

Criminal organizations frequently exploit global trade systems to move value around the world by employing complex and sometimes confusing documentation associated with legitimate trade transactions.

New Words

dismantle [dɪsˈmæntəl]

vt. 1) If you dismantle a machine or structure, you carefully separate it into its different parts. 拆除

E.g. Riot police responded with water cannon and tear gas to dismantle roadblocks on main streets.

2) To dismantle an organization or system means to cause it to stop functioning by gradually reducing its power or purpose. 逐步废除

E.g. We're building new partnerships around the world to disrupt, dismantle, and defeat al-Qaeda and its affiliates.

extradite [ˈɛkstrəˌdaɪt]

vt. If someone is extradited, they are officially sent back to their own or another country or state to be tried for a crime that they have been accused of. 引渡

E.g. Thai diplomats on Wednesday morning presented Cambodian officials with a request to detain and extradite Thaksin Shinawatra.

→派生词　extradition　[C,U]*n.* 引渡

E.g. He is currently in custody awaiting extradition to the U.S. for alleged terrorism offences.

incarcerate [ɪnˈkɑːsəˌreɪt]

vt. If people are incarcerated, they are kept in a prison or other place. [正式] 监禁

E.g. This effort should include immediate steps to apprehend and incarcerate terrorists operating within the PA's jurisdiction.

prosecution [ˌprɒsɪˈkjuːʃən]

[C]*n.* Prosecution is the action of charging someone with a crime and putting them on trial. 起诉

E.g. The head of government called for the prosecution of those responsible for the deaths.

[U]*n.* The lawyers who try to prove that a person on trial is guilty are called the prosecution. 原告律师

E.g. The prosecution claims Beard was using the assets of the charity for her own ends.

proponent [prəˈpəʊnənt]

[C]*n.* If you are a proponent of a particular idea or course of action, you actively support it. (某观念或行为的)支持者

E.g. He was identified as a leading proponent of the values of the university.

intimidate [ɪnˈtɪmɪˌdeɪt]

vt. If you intimidate someone, you deliberately make them frightened enough to do what you want them to do. 恐吓;威胁

E.g. Mr. Raffarin insists he will not allow the protesters to intimidate his government away from reform.

→派生词　intimidation　[U]*n.* 威胁

E.g. The European Union monitoring mission says the violence and intimidation prevented a free election in some parts of the country.

exemplary [ɪɡ'zɛmpləri]

adj. If you describe someone or something as exemplary, you think they are extremely good. 堪称典范的

E.g. And within that extraordinary institution, Justice Stevens has played a particularly distinguished and exemplary role.

narcotic [nɑː'kɒtɪk]

[C] *n.* Narcotics are drugs such as opium or heroin which make you sleepy and stop you from feeling pain. You can also use narcotics to mean any kind of illegal drugs. 麻醉剂;毒品

E.g. He was indicted for dealing in narcotics.

他因贩卖毒品而受到起诉。

adj. If something, especially a drug, has a narcotic effect, it makes the person who uses it feel sleepy. 麻醉的

E.g. ... hormones that have a narcotic effect on the immune system.

……对免疫系统有麻醉作用的激素。

anecdotal [ˌænɛk'dəʊtəl]

adj. Anecdotal evidence is based on individual accounts, rather than on reliable research or statistics, and so may not be valid. 轶闻的

E.g. Anecdotal evidence suggests these efforts have been effective.

overt ['əʊvɜːt]

adj. An overt action or attitude is done or shown in an open and obvious way. 公开的;明显的

E.g. As a third-generation Mexican-American growing up in Los Angeles, I had never encountered such overt racism.

sovereignty ['sɒvrəntɪ]

[U] *n.* Sovereignty is the power that a country has to govern itself or another country or state. 统治权

E.g. The issue of sovereignty over the islands remains a hot topic among many people.

indictment [ɪn'daɪtmənt]

[C] *n.* 1) If you say that one thing is an indictment of another thing, you mean that it shows how bad the other thing is. 控诉

E.g. The book is an indictment of the government.

2) An indictment is a formal accusation that someone has committed a crime. [法]控告

E.g. The Iraqi government said 17 civilians were killed, although the indictment alleges 14 died.

transparency [træns'pærənsɪ]

[C] *n.* A transparency is a small piece of photographic film with a frame around it which can be projected onto a screen so that you can see the picture. 幻灯片

[U] *n.* Transparency is the quality that an object or substance has when you can see through it. 透明性

E.g. And almost all of these reforms are designed to bring new transparency to campaign spending.

kingpin ['kɪŋˌpɪn]

[C] *n.* If you describe someone as the kingpin of an organization, you mean that they are the most important person involved in it. 关键人物

E.g. Mexico's top drug kingpin lord, who's reportedly 54, was captured in Guatemala in 1993, but escaped eight years later.

mandate ['mændeɪt]

[C] *n.* 1) If a government or other elected body has a mandate to carry out a particular policy or task, they have the authority to carry it out as a result of winning an election or vote. (政府或机构经选举而获得的)授权

E.g. It said the UK government had "absolutely no mandate" to change the voting system in Wales.

2) If someone is given a mandate to carry out a particular policy or task,

they are given the official authority to do it. （个人所获得的）授权

E.g. The independent prosecutor has a mandate to pursue this investigation.

3) You can refer to the fixed length of time that a country's leader or government remains in office as their mandate. [正式]任期

E.g. The president intended to leave politics once his mandate ends.

vt. 1) When someone is mandated to carry out a particular policy or task, they are given the official authority to do it. 授权

E.g. The police officer was mandated to investigate the case.

2) To mandate something means to make it mandatory. 强制执行

E.g. The government could mandate the new policy.

forfeiture [ˈfɔːfɪtʃə]

[U] *n.* Forfeiture is the action of forfeiting something. [法] （对某物的）没收

E.g. Asset forfeiture occurs when government seizes property that is associated with a crime.

incapacitate [ˌɪnkəˈpæsɪˌteɪt]

vt. If something incapacitates you, it weakens you in some way, so that you cannot do certain things. [正式]使……能力变弱；使伤残

E.g. But the instruction is not shoot to kill, the instruction is to immediately incapacitate the person.

infrastructure [ˈɪnfrəˌstrʌktʃə]

[C, U] *n.* The infrastructure of a country, society, or organization consists of the basic facilities such as transportation, communications, power supplies, and buildings, which enable it to function. （国家、社会、组织赖以行使职能的）基础设施

E.g. Beijing is co-operating with Islamabad on missile development, cross-border infrastructure and a deep-water port.

subvert [səbˈvɜːt]

vt. To subvert something means to destroy its power and influence. [正式]

颠覆

E.g. Hackers in Iran have been accused of trying to subvert one of the net's key security systems.

testimony [ˈtɛstɪmənɪ]

[C] *n.* In a court of law, someone's testimony is a formal statement that they make about what they saw someone do or what they know of a situation, after having promised to tell the truth. (法庭上的)证词

E.g. The testimony differed from prosecution witness Ronald Shipp, a former police officer and Simpson friend.

[U] *n.* If you say that one thing is testimony to another, you mean that it shows clearly that the second thing has a particular quality. 明证

E.g. The environmental movement is testimony to the widespread feelings of support for nature's importance.

Exercises

▶ Exercise One: Reading comprehension

Answer the following questions in your own words after reading the passage.

1. Please introduce the key U.S. foreign policy tools available for targeting major drug traffickers and their illicit networks.
2. How does the author define extradition? According to the proponents of extradition to the United States, what benefits does extradition bring while combating drug trafficking? And why do some countries refuse to extradite drug traffickers?
3. According to the passage, what measures does the U.S. adopt to combat money laundering?
4. Please list the U.S. agencies which are involved in counterdrug-related capacity building efforts abroad.
5. Please list the the U.S. agencies which are involved in providing anti-narcotics law

enforcement training, technical assistance, and equipment for foreign personnel.

▶ Exercise Two: Translation

Please translate the following sentences into Chinese.

1. Key U.S. foreign policy tools available for targeting major drug traffickers and their illicit networks include establishing extradition agreements with foreign countries, freezing and blocking foreign criminal assets within U.S. jurisdiction, and building foreign capacity to investigate, arrest, prosecute, and incarcerate drug traffickers domestically.
2. Proponents of extradition to the United States argue that suspected criminals are more likely to receive a fair trial in U.S. courts than in countries where the local judicial process may be corrupt and where suspects can use bribes and intimidation to manipulate the outcome of a trial.
3. Currently, several U.S. agencies are involved in international anti-money laundering efforts designed to enhance financial transaction transparency and regulation, improve cooperation and coordination with foreign governments and private financial institutions, and provide foreign countries with law enforcement training and support.
4. Further, emerging challenges include the growing volume of financial transactions, especially the volume of international electronic transfers, and the movement of illegal money laundering outside formal banking channels, including through "hawala"-type chains of transnational money brokers and through the use of stored-value cards.

Part Ⅱ After-class Reading

Text B

Against Drug Threat
—*International Law Enforcement Agencies in Concert*

Drug trafficking has become one of the major criminal activities of organised crime groups that plan, operate and control the deals across national boundaries. Transnational drug crimes attract the attention of law enforcement agencies of all countries and places as illicit drug markets know no borders and their transnational nature puts them beyond the reach of any single government, rich or poor. It is imperative for effective and strong enforcement mechanisms to be set up to suppress the problems. In realising that ultimate success in the eradication of drug crimes requires determined, effective and coordinated action at the international level, Hong Kong Customs accords very high priority to international cooperation and maintains close links with the work partners around the world in any joint investigation to meet its obligations in anti-drug work.

International Framework and Multilateral Agreements

Hong Kong is committed to concerted international efforts in combating illicit drug trafficking. At present, three major international anti-drug conventions apply to Hong Kong, namely the 1961 Single Convention on Narcotic Drugs as amended by the Protocol of 1972, the 1971 Convention on Psychotropic Substances, and the 1988 United Nations Convention against Illicit Traffic in Narcotic Drugs and Psychotropic Substances. The conventions provide a treaty-based framework for international cooperation to address the drug problem. They also involve the assumption of responsibilities in formulating domestic anti-drug policy.

While the cross-border dimension of drug trafficking has been understood and translated into a highly developed system of international cooperation, the opening up of global markets has heightened its significance. More than ever, Hong Kong recognises that a multilateral and coordinated response is needed to tackle drug activities. To strengthen multilateral cooperation to combat transnational crimes and drug trafficking activities, Hong Kong has signed Mutual Legal Assistance in Criminal Matters Agreements with 15 countries and Surrender of Fugitive Offenders Agreements with 13 countries. In addition, a number of agreements are currently under discussion. The agreements form the base to secure better coordination and cooperation.

Law Enforcement Agencies in Concert

To promote closer participation and assistance across state and territory wide jurisdictions in the international anti-drug arena, law enforcement agencies are taking active steps to surmount difficulties, which include lack of cooperation agreements, lack of proper joint operation procedures, insufficient trust between countries due to historical or political reasons, different legal systems, language barriers, etc.

Hong Kong has also made great efforts in the fight against transnational drug trafficking activities, which resulted in diminishing its role as a drug transiting centre over the past years.

As external cooperation is one of the anti-drug strategies to restrict drug supply, Hong Kong, being a prime player in the drug war, has adopted a collaborative approach at the international level. From time to time, we conduct joint operations with our counterparts, which culminate in prominent results. In the following paragraphs, we illustrate two successful examples.

Operation "Cold Remedy"

This is a multi-agency operation among Hong Kong Customs, Department of Health of Hong Kong, the U.S. DEA/HKCO and other overseas authorities to monitor the export of pseudoephedrine, a precursor chemical for the production of methamphetamine. The operation was initiated when four shipments of 19.2 million cold tablets containing pseudoephedrine were seized in the US, Panama and Mexico in early 2003. The shipments were exported under valid licences issued by Department of Health. There was evidence that drug traffickers imported these pseudoephedrine preparations and illegally diverted them to the clandestine laboratories for conversion into methamphetamine, destined for the U.S. market. Intelligence also showed it was a new trend that traffickers in Mexico made use of fictitious importers to source pseudoephedrine combination products for illicit manufacturing of methamphetamine.

To suppress the emerging trend, Hong Kong Customs, in collaboration with Department of Health and U.S. DEA launched a joint operation coded "Cold Remedy" commencing from July 2003 to monitor export shipments of pseudoephedrine tablets. Under the joint operation, Department of Health would screen all export licences and identify those shipments involving pseudoephedrine tablets for Hong Kong Customs and the U.S. DEA's profiling and monitoring respectively. U.S. DEA would coordinate with Mexican and Panamanian authorities as well as other concerned countries through their network for tracing the movement of targeted shipments and planning enforcement actions.

To ensure timely exchange and effective use of intelligence, efficient monitoring of suspicious pseudoephedrine shipments and taking of appropriate enforcement actions, a number of initiatives had been taken which included the following:

(a) setting up contact points for constant and immediate

communication;

(b) involving high level officials to show commitment of participating agencies and achieve better decision making;

(c) joint-agency approach to enhance information assessment for improved intelligence dissemination in supporting the operation; and

(d) regular operational meetings between concerned parties to review progress, strategy and resource deployment. (Note: two meetings had been held in Washington DC, with the attendance of senior officials of Hong Kong Customs, Department of Health of Hong Kong, U.S. DEA and Mexican authorities.)

During the 16-month operation, there were nine cases effected in Mexico and the U.S. with a total seizure of 66 million pseudoephedrine combination tablets and 19 arrests made by the Mexican U.S. authorities between September 2003 and December 2004. After a series of stringent enforcement actions taken in Central and North America, diversion activities have severely been curtailed. Intelligence indicated that drug syndicates have refrained from involving Hong Kong as a source of pseudoephedrine preparations for their clandestine manufacture of methamphetamine.

Admittedly, multi-agency cooperation is the key to success in this operation. Recognising it as a very effective tool in preventing pseudoephedrine preparation diversions, DEA HQ launched an initiative to request all their country offices to introduce the model to their host countries to share the efficient practices and work together to stop the trend. While sharing Hong Kong's exemplary experience, all concerned parties agreed to extend Operation "Cold Remedy" to ensure that the trend would not revive.

Operation "Tsunami"

Operation "Tsunami" is a joint operation between Hong Kong Customs and the Anti-smuggling Bureau of Shenzhen Customs to neutralise cross-boundary drug trafficking syndicates. Over the past years, Hong Kong-China based drug syndicates operated their drug manufactories and manned the drug storages in Mainland China. Traffickers only brought small quantities of drug into Hong Kong through the boundary control points to meet the demand of the local market. Intelligence revealed many of the trafficking activities were concentrated in Guangdong province, in particular, cities close to Hong Kong. In view of the modus operandi, Hong Kong Customs deployed more resources to focus on cross-boundary traffickers. The intelligence-driven operations often resulted in seizures and arrests. Despite successful interdiction of drug smuggling activities, it was not too often that high level syndicate members were netted and we could hardly get hold of their activities once they crossed the control point. With insufficient intelligence in hand, investigation became a tough job to law enforcers.

Understanding that organised crimes are evolving and we must accelerate our paces to cope with the situation, Hong Kong Customs has established cooperative mechanisms with the Anti-smuggling Bureau of Shenzhen Customs under a joint operation codenamed Operation "Tsunami" since 1 April 2004, in an effort to combat cross-boundary trafficking activities. The scope of cooperation included exchange of intelligence, assistance in investigation and mounting of synchronised operations. Through the gathering of ideas and experiences, joint intelligence analysis and field study, we found out the operational limitations and enforcement loopholes. The joint venture contributed a harmonised thinking and both eventually worked out an effective plan to overcome the hurdles.

Operation "Tsunami", representing a strengthened cooperation of law enforcers, proved to be highly successful. As a result of intelligence exchange, joint movement monitoring and continuous surveillance on the key targets mounted in Hong Kong and on the Mainland, together with a series of raiding operations, two Hong Kong-China based drug syndicates involved in drug manufacturing and cross-boundary trafficking acts were crushed in May and July of 2004. Smashing one clandestine laboratory, officers of the Anti-smuggling Bureau of Shenzhen Customs arrested 20 high and mid level syndicate members and seized 16.4 kilograms of heroin, 2,600 tablets of MDMA and 1.2 kilograms of assorted drugs/chemicals, with drug proceeds amounting to HK $450,000.

The success of Operation "Tsunami" demonstrates not only the ever closer partnership with our Mainland counterparts, but also the strong commitments and determination of both sides in tackling cross-boundary drug trafficking rings. More essentially, the operation brings long-term benefits by showing a joint striking force with an enhanced deterrent effect on transnational drug deals.

The Way Forward

Drug trafficking is a global shared problem that brings threat to every country. To counteract the increase of collaboration among transnational criminal groups, law enforcement officers must work in alliance beyond the territory boundaries for the common goal. It is the assertive anti-drug policy of the Hong Kong SAR Government to be fully committed to international cooperation against drug threat at all fronts.

(1,469 words)

Unit 5

Cyber-crime

Part Ⅰ In-class Reading

Pre-reading Questions

- *Have you ever heard of cyber-crime before? Do you think it is a quite serious problem which should be promptly tackled?*
- *Could you present some reasons why cyber-crime is wildly spread around the world?*
- *What factors do you think increase the difficulties of combating cyber-crime for the law enforcement officers in the world?*

Text A

Manhattan U.S. Attorney and FBI Assistant Director in Charge Announce 24 Arrests in Eight Countries as Part of International Cyber Crime Takedown (Part One)

Two-Year FBI Undercover "Carding" Operation Protected Over 400,000 Potential Cyber Crime Victims and Prevented Over $205 Million in Losses

Preet Bharara, the United States Attorney for the Southern District of New York, and Janice K. Fedarcyk, the Assistant Director in Charge of the New York Field Office of the Federal Bureau of Investigation (FBI), announced today the largest coordinated international law enforcement action in history directed at "carding" crimes—offenses in which the Internet is used to traffic in and exploit the stolen credit card, bank account, and other personal identification information of hundreds of thousands of victims globally. Today's coordinated action—involving 13 countries, including the United States—resulted in 24 arrests, including the domestic arrests of 11 individuals by federal and local authorities in the United States, and the arrests of 13 individuals abroad by foreign law enforcement in seven countries. In addition, the federal and local authorities and authorities overseas today conducted more than 30 subject interviews and executed more than 30 search warrants. Today's coordinated actions result from a two-year undercover operation led by the FBI that was designed to locate cyber-criminals, investigate and expose them, and disrupt their activities.

Eleven individuals were arrested today, and one last night, in the United States: Christian Cangeopol, a/k/a "404myth", was arrested today in Lawrenceville, Georgia; Mark Caparelli, a/k/a "Cubby", was arrested in San Diego, California; Sean Harper, a/k/a "Kabraxis314", was arrested in Albuquerque, New Mexico; Alex Hatala, a/k/a "kool+kake", was arrested in Jacksonville, Florida; Joshua Hicks, a/k/a "OxideDox", was arrested in Bronx, New York; Michael Hogue, a/k/a "xVisceral", was arrested in Tucson, Arizona; Mir Islam, a/k/a "JoshTheGod", was arrested in Manhattan, New York; Peter Ketchum, a/k/a "IwearaMAGNUM", was arrested in Pittsfield, Massachusetts; Steven Hansen, a/k/a "theboner1", was arrested in Wisconsin, where he is currently serving a prison sentence on state charges. In addition, two minors, whose names will not be made public, were arrested by local authorities in Long Beach and Sacramento, California.

Hicks and Islam will be presented later today before a magistrate judge in the Southern District of New York. The other federally arrested defendants will be presented before magistrate judges in the corresponding federal districts of arrest.

Another 13 individuals were arrested today in seven foreign countries. Eleven of those individuals were arrested as a result of investigations commenced in foreign jurisdictions based in part on information arising out of the undercover operation and provided by the FBI to foreign law enforcement. Those 11 arrests occurred in the United Kingdom (6), Bosnia (2), Bulgaria (1), Norway (1), and Germany (1). Two additional defendants were arrested today in foreign countries based on provisional arrest warrants obtained by the United States in connection with complaints unsealed today in the Southern District of New York. Those two individuals are Ali Hassan, a/k/a/"Badoo", who was arrested in Italy; and Lee Jason Juesheng, a/k/a "iAlert", or "Jason Kato", who was arrested in Japan. Australia, Canada, Denmark, and Macedonia conducted interviews, executed search warrants, or took other coordinated action in connection with today's takedown.

Charges were also unsealed in the Southern District of New York against four additional defendants who remain at large.

Manhattan U.S. Attorney Preet Bharara said, "As the cyber threat grows more international, the response must be increasingly global and forceful. The coordinated law enforcement actions taken by an unprecedented number of countries around the world today demonstrate that hackers and fraudsters cannot count on being able to prowl the Internet in anonymity and with impunity, even across national boundaries. Clever computer criminals operating behind the supposed veil of the Internet are still subject to the long arm of the law.

The allegations unsealed today chronicle a breathtaking spectrum of cyber schemes and scams. As described in the charging documents, individuals sold credit cards by the thousands and took the private information of untold numbers of people. As alleged, the defendants casually offered every stripe of malware and virus to fellow fraudsters, even including software-enabling cyber voyeurs to hijack an unsuspecting consumer's personal computer camera. To expose and prosecute individuals like the alleged cyber-criminals charged today will continue to require exactly the kind of coordinated response and international cooperation that made today's arrests possible.

FBI Assistant Director in Charge Janice K. Fedarcyk said, "From New York to Norway and Japan to Australia, Operation Card Shop targeted sophisticated, highly organized cyber-criminals involved in buying and selling stolen identities, exploited credit cards, counterfeit documents, and sophisticated hacking tools. Spanning four continents, the two-year undercover FBI investigation is the latest example of our commitment to rooting out rampant criminal behavior on the Internet. Cyber-crooks trade contraband and advance their schemes online with impunity, and they will only be stopped by law enforcement's continued vigilance and cooperation. Today's arrests cause significant disruption to the underground economy and are a stark reminder that masked IP addresses and private forums are no sanctuary for criminals and are not beyond the reach of the FBI."

Background on Carding Crimes

"Carding" refers to various criminal activities associated with stealing personal identification information and financial information belonging to other individuals—including the account information associated with credit cards, bank cards, debit cards, or other access devices—and using that information to obtain money, goods, or services without the victims' authorization or consent. For example, a criminal might gain unauthorized access to (or "hack") a database maintained on a computer server and steal credit card numbers and other personal information stored in that database. The criminal can then use the stolen information to, among other things, buy goods or services online; manufacture counterfeit credit cards by encoding them with the stolen account information; manufacture false identification documents (which can be used in turn to facilitate fraudulent purchases); or sell the stolen information to others who intend to use it for criminal purposes. Carding refers to the foregoing criminal activity generally and encompasses a variety of federal offenses, including, but not limited to, identification document fraud, aggravated identity theft, access device fraud, computer hacking, and wire fraud.

"Carding forums" are websites used by criminals engaged in carding ("carders") to facilitate their criminal activity. Carders use carding forums to, among other things, exchange information related to carding, such as information concerning hacking methods or computer-security vulnerabilities that could be used to obtain personal identification information; and to buy and sell goods and services related to carding—for example, stolen credit or debit card account numbers, hardware for creating counterfeit credit or debit cards, or goods bought with compromised credit card or debit card accounts. Carding forums often permit users to post public messages—postings that can be viewed by all users of the site—sometimes referred to as threads. For example, a user who has stolen credit card numbers may post a public thread offering to sell the numbers. Carding forums also often permit users to communicate one-to-one through so-called private messages. Because carding forums are, in essence, marketplaces for illegal activities, access is typically restricted to avoid law enforcement surveillance. Typically, a prospective user seeking to join a carding forum can only do so if other, already established users vouch for him or her, or if he or she pays a sum of money to the operators of the carding forum. User accounts are typically identified by a username and the access is restricted by password. Users of carding forums typically identify themselves on such forums using aliases or online nicknames ("nics").

Individuals who use stolen credit card information to purchase goods on the Internet are typically reluctant to ship the goods to their own home addresses, for fear that law enforcement could easily trace the purchases. Accordingly, carders often seek out "drop addresses"—addresses with which they have no association, such as vacant houses or apartments—where carded goods can be shipped and retrieved without leaving evidence of their involvement in the shipment. Some individuals used carding forums to sell "drop services" to other forum members, usually in exchange for some form of compensation. One frequently used form of compensation is a "1-to-1" arrangement in which the carder wishing to ship to the drop must ship two of whatever items he has carded—one for the provider of the drop to forward to the carder and the other for the provider of the drop to keep as payment in kind for the carder's use of the drop. Another frequently used compensation arrangement is for the carder and the drop provider to agree to resell the carded items shipped to the drop and to split the proceeds between them.

Background on the Undercover Operation

In June 2010, the FBI established an undercover carding forum called "Carder Profit" (the "UC Site"), enabling users to discuss various topics related to carding and to communicate offers to buy, sell, and exchange goods and services related to carding, among other things. Since individuals engaged in these unlawful activities on one of many other carding websites on the Internet, the FBI established the UC Site in an effort to identify these cyber-criminals, investigate their crimes, and prevent harm to innocent victims. The UC Site was configured to allow the FBI to monitor and to record the discussion threads posted to the site, as well as private messages sent through the site between registered users. The UC Site also allowed the

FBI to record the Internet Protocol (IP) addresses of users' computers when they accessed the site. The IP address is the unique number that identifies a computer on the Internet and allows information to be routed properly between computers.

Access to the UC Site, which was taken offline in May 2012, was limited to registered members and required a username and password to gain entry. Various membership requirements were imposed from time to time to restrict site membership to individuals with established knowledge of carding techniques or interest in criminal activity. For example, at times, new users were prevented from joining the site unless they were recommended by two existing users who had registered with the site or unless they paid a registration fee.

New users registering with the UC Site were required to provide a valid e-mail address as part of the registration process. The e-mail addresses entered by registered members of the site were collected by the FBI.

(1,691 words)

Background Information

▶ FBI

The Federal Bureau of Investigation (FBI) is a governmental agency belonging to the United States Department of Justice. The bureau was established in 1908 as the Bureau of Investigation (BOI). Its name was changed to the Federal Bureau of Investigation (FBI) in 1935. The FBI headquarters is the J. Edgar Hoover Building, located in Washington, D.C. The bureau has fifty-six field offices located in major cities throughout the United States, and more than 400 resident agencies in lesser cities and areas across the nation. More than 50 international offices called "legal attachés" exist in U.S. embassies and consulates general worldwide.

As an intelligence-driven and a threat-focused national security organization with both intelligence and law enforcement responsibilities, the mission of the FBI is to protect and defend the United States against terrorist and foreign intelligence threats, to uphold and enforce the criminal laws of the United States, and to provide leadership and criminal justice services to federal, state, municipal, and international agencies and partners.

▶ a/k/a

"Also known as", used to introduce pseudonyms, aliases, nicknames, working names, legalized names, pen names, maiden names, etc.

▶ IP

The Internet Protocol (IP) is the principal communications protocol in the Internet protocol suite for relaying datagrams across network boundaries. Its routing function enables internetworking, and essentially establishes the Internet.

IP, as the primary protocol in the Internet layer of the Internet protocol suite, has the task of delivering packets from the source host to the destination host solely based on the IP addresses in the packet headers. For this purpose, IP defines packet structures that encapsulate the data to be delivered. It also defines addressing methods that are used to label the datagram with source and destination information.

New Words

attorney [əˈtɜːnɪ]

[C] *n.* In the United States, an attorney or attorney-at-law is a lawyer. 律师

E.g. At the hearing, her attorney did not enter a plea.

warrant [ˈwɒrənt]

vt. If something warrants a particular action, it makes the action seem necessary or appropriate for the circumstances. 使……显得必要;使……显得适当

E.g. The allegations are serious enough to warrant an investigation.

[C] *n.* A warrant is a legal document that allows someone to do something, especially one that is signed by a judge or magistrate and gives the police permission to arrest someone or search their house. 搜查令;拘捕令

E.g. After his arrest, investigators obtained a search warrant and collected a DNA sample from Biela.

magistrate [ˈmædʒɪˌstreɪt]

[C] *n.* A magistrate is an official who acts as a judge in law courts which deal with minor crimes or disputes. 治安法官

E.g. "Tell us what it is you want, and do not interrupt the court," said the magistrate.

defendant [dɪˈfɛndənt]

[C] *n.* A defendant is a person who has been accused of breaking the law and is being tried in court. 被告

E.g. As part of the agreement, the defendant agreed to waive any rights of appeal.

provisional [prəˈvɪʒənəl]

adj. You use provisional to describe something that has been arranged or appointed for the present, but may be changed in the future. 临时的;暂时的

E.g. The statistics are provisional and the final version will be published in March next year.

unprecedented [ʌnˈprɛsɪˌdɛntɪd]

adj. If something is unprecedented, it has never happened before. 史无前例的

E.g. Vice president Ronnie Nathanielz credits his company with raising the popularity of basketball to unprecedented levels.

hacker [ˈhækə]

[C] *n.* 1) A computer hacker is someone who tries to break into computer systems, especially in order to get secret information. (电脑)黑客

E.g. They are looking for a computer hacker who has downloaded thousands of credit card numbers.

2) A computer hacker is someone who uses a computer a lot, especially so much that they have no time to do anything else. 计算机迷

fraudster [ˈfrɔːdstə]

[C] *n.* a swindler 骗子

E.g. Disturbingly, a card receipt is all a clever fraudster needs to reproduce a replica card.

prowl [praʊl]

vi. If an animal or a person prowls around, they move around quietly, for example, when they are hunting. 悄悄巡行

E.g. He prowled around the room, not sure what he was looking for or even why he was there.

anonymity [ˌænəˈnɪmətɪ]

[U] *n.* the state of remaining unknown to most other people

E.g. Anyone providing information to the police will be guaranteed anonymity.

impunity [ɪmˈpjuːnɪtɪ]

[U] *n.* If you say that someone does something with impunity, you disapprove of the fact that they are not punished for doing something bad. 不受惩罚

E.g. No nation, large or small, can violate the rights of its citizens with impunity.

allegation [ˌælɪˈgeɪʃən]

[C] *n.* An allegation is a statement saying that someone has done something wrong. 指控

E.g. Pakistan rejected the allegation, saying there was no evidence that its intelligence staff were involved.

chronicle [ˈkrɒnɪkəl]

vt. To chronicle a series of events means to write about them or show them in broadcasts in the order in which they happened. 按发生时间顺序编写或播放

E.g. We've decided to chronicle its 15 greatest moments here.

[C] *n.* A chronicle is an account or record of a series of events. 编年史

E.g. ... this vast chronicle of the Qing Dynasty.

malware [ˈmælwεə]

[C] *n.* a computer program designed specifically to damage or disrupt a system, such as a virus 恶意软件

E.g. In my opinion, such an agency should focus only on fighting international malware crime gangs.

voyeur [vwɑɪˈɜː, vɔˈɪ-]

[C] *n.* 1) A voyeur is someone who gets sexual pleasure from secretly watching other people having sex or taking their clothes off. 窥淫癖者

2) If you describe someone as a voyeur, you disapprove of them because you think they enjoy watching other people's suffering or problems. 好刺探他人隐私者

E.g. The media has made unfeeling voyeurs of all of us.

rampant [ˈræmpənt]

adj. If you describe something bad, such as a crime or disease, as rampant, you mean that it is very common and is increasing in an uncontrolled way. 猖獗的;泛滥的

E.g. Voters also complain about rampant corruption among local authorities.

crook [krʊk]

[C] *n.* A crook is a dishonest person or a criminal. [非正式]无赖;恶棍

E.g. The man is a crook and a liar.

contraband [ˈkɒntrəˌbænd]

[U] *n.* Contraband refers to goods that are taken into or out of a country illegally. 走私品

E.g. Security Council passed a resolution June 12 calling on all states to inspect vessels suspected of containing contraband.

vigilant [ˈvɪdʒɪlənt]

adj. Someone who is vigilant gives careful attention to a particular problem or situation and concentrates on noticing any danger or trouble that there might be. 警惕的

E.g. In terms of self-protection, the Home Office advises the public to be above all vigilant.

→派生词 vigilance [U] *n.* 警惕

E.g. We are protected from attack only by vigorous action abroad and increased vigilance at home.

stark [stɑːk]

adj. 1) Stark choices or statements are harsh and unpleasant. 严酷的

E.g. The stark fact is that Japanese manufactures threaten American products more than Chinese products.

2) If two things are in stark contrast to one another, they are very different from each other in a way that is very obvious. (对比)鲜明的

E.g. These setbacks in central Africa are in stark contrast to improvements elsewhere on the continent.

sanctuary [ˈsæŋktjʊərɪ]

[C] *n.* A sanctuary is a place where people who are in danger from other people can go to be safe. 避难所

E.g. For 46 years, the Jigokudani Monkey Park has been a sanctuary for these snow monkeys.

[U] *n.* Sanctuary is the safety provided in a sanctuary. 庇护

E.g. The broads provide a sanctuary for all types of wildlife.

encode [ɪnˈkəʊd]

vt. If you encode a message or some information, you put it into a code or express it in a different form or system of language. 将……写为密码

E.g. The two parties encode confidential data in a form that is not directly readable by the other party.

双方把机密数据写成一种不能被对方直接读懂的密码。

encompass [ɪn'kʌmpəs]

vt. 1) If something encompasses particular things, it includes them. 包含

E.g. Cultures encompass not only art and literature, but also lifestyles, value systems, traditions and beliefs.

2) To encompass a place means to completely surround or cover it. 围住;覆盖

E.g. The fog soon encompassed the whole valley.

alias ['eɪlɪəs]

[C] *n.* An alias is a false name, especially one used by a criminal. 化名

E.g. Using an alias, he had lived there for more than three years.

prep. You use alias when you are mentioning another name that someone, especially a criminal or an actor, is known by. 化名为

E.g. Mr Harrison—whose alias was "Yupo"—was arrested in the city of Apatzingan in Michoacan.

compensation [kɒmpɛn'seɪʃən]

[U] *n.* Compensation is money that someone who has experienced loss or suffering claims from the person or organization responsible, or from the state. 补偿金

E.g. Mr Smith is applying for compensation from West Midlands Police Authority.

[C, U] *n.* If something is some compensation for something bad that has happened, it makes you feel better. 补偿

E.g. I wish I were young again, but getting older has its compensations.

configure [kən'fɪgə]

vt. If you configure a piece of computer equipment, you set it up so that it is ready for use. 配置(计算机设备)

E.g. It lets you have multiple virtual desktops, which you can configure to suit different needs.

protocol [ˈprəʊtəˌkɒl]

[C,U] *n.* Protocol is a system of rules about the correct way to act in formal situations. 礼节

E.g. the protocol of diplomatic visits

[C] *n.* 1) A protocol is a set of rules for exchanging information between computers. (计算机间交换信息的)协议

2) A protocol is a written record of a treaty or agreement that has been made by two or more countries. 议定书

E.g. Thus, representatives from 160 nations gathered last December to hammer out the Kyoto Protocol.

3) A protocol is a plan for a course of medical treatment, or a plan for a scientific experiment. 医疗方案;科学试验计划

E.g. ... the detoxification protocol.

Exercises

▶ Exercise One: Reading comprehension

Answer the following questions in your own words after reading the passage.

1. What is carding crime according to the passage?
2. What do the alleged cyber criminals mentioned in the passage casually do to conduct cyber crimes?
3. After reading the passage, what do you know about "carding forums"? What do they mean to the cyber criminals?
4. What are "drop addresses"? What benefits do they bring to the cyber criminals?
5. What role does the UC Site established by the FBI play when combating carding crime?

▶ Exercise Two: Translation

Please translate the following sentences into Chinese.

1. Preet Bharara, the United States Attorney for the Southern District of New York, and Janice K. Fedarcyk, the Assistant Director in Charge of the New York Field Office of the Federal Bureau of Investigation (FBI), announced today the largest coordinated international law enforcement action in history directed at "carding" crimes—offenses in which the Internet is used to traffic in and exploit the stolen credit card, bank account, and other personal identification information of hundreds of thousands of victims globally.
2. The coordinated law enforcement actions taken by an unprecedented number of countries around the world today demonstrate that hackers and fraudsters cannot count on being able to prowl the Internet in anonymity and with impunity, even across national boundaries. Clever computer criminals operating behind the supposed veil of the Internet are still subject to the long arm of the law. From New York to Norway and Japan to Australia, Operation Card Shop targeted sophisticated, highly organized cyber criminals involved in buying and selling stolen identities, exploited credit cards, counterfeit documents, and sophisticated hacking tools. Spanning four continents, the two-year undercover FBI investigation is the latest example of our commitment to rooting out rampant criminal behavior on the Internet.
3. "Carding" refers to various criminal activities associated with stealing personal identification information and financial information belonging to other individuals—including the account information associated with credit cards, bank cards, debit cards, or other access devices—and using that information to obtain money, goods, or services without the victims' authorization or consent.
4. Carding refers to the foregoing criminal activity generally and encompasses a variety of federal offenses, including, but not limited to, identification document fraud, aggravated identity theft, access device fraud, computer hacking, and wire fraud.

Part Ⅱ After-class Reading

Text B

Manhattan U.S. Attorney and FBI Assistant Director in Charge Announce 24 Arrests in Eight Countries as Part of International Cyber Crime Takedown (Part Two)

Two-Year FBI Undercover "Carding" Operation Protected Over 400,000 Potential Cyber Crime Victims and Prevented Over $205 Million in Losses

Harm Prevented by the Undercover Operation

In the course of the undercover operation, the FBI contacted multiple affected institutions and/or individuals to advise them of discovered breaches in order to enable them to take appropriate responsive and protective measures. In doing so, the FBI has prevented estimated potential economic losses of more than $205 million, notified credit card providers of over 411,000 compromised credit and debit cards, and notified 47 companies, government entities, and educational institutions of the breach of their networks.

The Charged Conduct

As alleged in the complaints unsealed today in the Southern District of New York, the defendants are charged with engaging in a variety of online carding offenses in which they sought to profit through, among other means, the sale of hacked victim account information, personal identification information, hacking tools, drop services, and other services that could facilitate carding activity.

Michael Hogue, a/k/a "xVisceral," offered malware for sale, including remote access tools (RATs) that allowed the user to take over and remotely control the operations of an infected victim-computer. Hogue's RAT, for example, enabled the user to turn on the web camera on victims' computers to spy on them and to record every keystroke of the victim-computer's user. If the victim visited a banking website and entered his or her user name and password, the key logging program could record that information, which could then be used to access the victim's bank account. Hogue sold his RAT widely over the Internet, usually for $50 per copy and boasted that he had personally infected "50—100" computers with his RAT and that he'd sold it to others who had infected "thousands" of computers with malware. Hogue's RAT infected computers in the United States, Canada, Germany, Denmark, Poland, and possibly other countries.

Jarand Moen Romtveit, a/k/a "zer0", used hacking tools to steal information from the internal databases of a bank, a hotel, and various online retailers, and then sold the information to others. In February 2012, in return for a laptop computer, Romtveit sold credit card information to an individual he believed to be a fellow carder, but who, in fact, was an undercover FBI agent.

Mir Islam, a/k/a "JoshTheGod", trafficked in stolen credit card information and possessed information for more than 50,000 credit cards. Islam also held himself out as a member of "UGNazi", a hacking group that has claimed credit for numerous recent online hacks, and as a founder of "Carders. Org", a carding forum on the Internet. Last night, Islam met in Manhattan with an individual he believed to be a fellow carder—but who, in fact, was an undercover FBI agent—to accept delivery of what Islam believed were counterfeit credit cards encoded with stolen credit card information. Islam was placed under arrest after he attempted to withdraw illicit proceeds from an ATM using one of the cards. Today, the FBI seized the web server for UGNazi.com and seized the domain name of Carders.org, taking both sites offline.

Steven Hansen, a/k/a "theboner1", and Alex Hatala, a/k/a "kool + kake", sold stolen CVVs, a term used by carders to refer to credit card data that includes the name, address, and zip code of the card holder, along with the card number, expiration date, and security code printed on the card. Hatala advertised to fellow carders that he got "fresh" CVVs on a "daily" basis from hacking into "DBs [databases] around the world".

Ali Hassan, a/k/a "Badoo", also sold "fulls", a term used by carders to refer to full credit card data including cardholder name, address, Social Security number, birthdate, mother's maiden name, and bank account information. Hassan claimed to have obtained at least some of them by having hacked into an online hotel booking site.

Joshua Hicks, a/k/a "OxideDox", and Lee Jason Jeusheng, a/k/a "iAlert" or "Jason Kato", each sold "dumps", which is a term used by carders to refer to stolen credit card data in a form in which the data is stored on the magnetic strips on the backs of credit cards. Hicks sold 15 credit card dumps in return for a camera and $250 in cash to a fellow carder who, unbeknownst to Hicks, was an undercover FBI agent. Hicks met the undercover agent in downtown Manhattan to consummate the sale. Similarly, Jeusheng sold 119 credit card dumps in return for three iPad 2s to a carder who was an undercover FBI agent. Jeusheng provided his shipping address in Japan to the undercover agent, which in part led to his identification and arrest.

Mark Caparelli, a/k/a "Cubby", engaged in a so-called "Apple call-in" scheme in which he used stolen credit cards and social engineering skills to fraudulently obtain replacement products from Apple Inc., which he then resold for profit. The scheme involved Caparelli obtaining serial numbers of

Apple products he had not bought. He would then call Apple with the serial number, claim the product was defective, arrange for a replacement product to be sent to an address he designated, and give Apple a stolen credit card number to charge if he failed to return the purportedly defective product. Caparelli sold and shipped four iPhone 4 cell phones that he had stolen through the Apple call-in scheme to an individual whom he believed to be a fellow-carder, but who, in fact, was an undercover FBI agent.

Sean Harper, a/k/a "Kabraxis 314", and Peter Ketchum, a/k/a "iwearaMAGNUM", each sold drop services to other carders in return for money or carded merchandise. Harper provided drop addresses in Albuquerque, New Mexico, to which co-conspirators sent expensive electronics, jewelry, and clothing, among other things. Ketchum advertised drop locations "spread across multiple cities" in the United States and allegedly received and shipped carded merchandise including sunglasses and air purifiers, as well as synthetic marijuana.

Christian Cangeopol, a/k/a "404myth", engaged in illegal "instoring" at Walmart to obtain Apple electronic devices with stolen credit cards. Instoring is a term used by carders to refer to using stolen credit card accounts to make in-store, as opposed to online, purchases of items using stolen credit card information and matching fake identifications. As part of the alleged scheme, Cangeopol and a co-conspirator used stolen credit card data to order electronic devices on Walmart's website; in selecting a delivery option, they opted to have items delivered to various Walmart stores in Georgia; Cangeopol then picked up the items using a fake identification; Cangeopol and the co-conspirator then resold the carded electronics and split the proceeds.

The attached chart reflects the name, age, residence of, and pending charges against each individual charged in the Southern District of New York.

List of Arrested Defendants Charged in SDNY Complaints

Defendant	SDNY Complaint Numer	Residence	Age	Charges and Maximum Penalties
Christian Cangeopol, a/k/a "404myth"	12 Mag. 1667	Lawrenceville, Georgia	19	Conspiracy to commit access device fraud (7.5 years in prison)
Mark Caparelli, a/k/a "Cubby"	12 Mag. 1640	San Diego, California	20	Wire fraud (20 years in prison) Access device fraud (10 years in prison)
Steven Hansen, a/k/a "theboner1"	12 Mag. 1641	Kentucky (in prison in Wisconsin)	23	Fraud in connection with identification information (Five years in prison)
Sean Harper, a/k/a "Kabraxis314"	12 Mag. 1638	Albuquerque, New Mexico	23	Conspiracy to commit access device fraud (7.5 years in prison)
Ali Hassan, a/k/a "Mr Badoo", "Mr. Badoo", or "Badoo"	12 Mag. 1565	Milan, Italy	22	Conspiracy to commit wire fraud (20 years in prison) Conspiracy to commit access device fraud, with object of possession 15 or more access devices (Five years in prison) Aggravated identity theft (Two years mandatory consecutive in prison)
Alex Hatala, a/k/a "kool+kake"	12 Mag. 1669	Jacksonville, Florida	19	Fraud in connection with identification information (Five years in prison)
Joshua Hicks, a/k/a "OxideDox"	12 Mag. 1639	Bronx, New York	19	Access device fraud (10 years in prison)
Michael Hogue, a/k/a "xVisceral"	12 Mag. 1632	Tucson, Arizona	21	Conspiracy to commit computer hacking (10 years in prison) Distribution of malware (10 years in prison)
Lee Jason Juesheng, a/k/a "iAlert", or "Jason Kato"	12 Mag. 1605	Tokyo, Japan	23	Access device fraud (10 years in prison)

(Continued)

Defendant	SDNY Complaint Numer	Residence	Age	Charges and Maximum Penalties
Peter Ketchum, Jr., a/k/a "iwearaMAGNUM"	12 Mag. 1651	Pittsfield, Massachusetts	21	Conspiracy to commit access device fraud (7.5 years in prison)
Jarand Moen Romtveit, a/k/a "zer0", or "zer0iq"	12 Mag. 1656	Porsgrunn, Norway	25	Access device fraud (possession 15 unauthorized devices) (10 years in prison) Access device fraud (affecting transactions with unauthorized devices) (15 years in prison) Aggravated identity theft (Two years mandatory, consecutive in prison)
Mir Islam, a/k/a "JoshTheGod"	—	Bronx, New York	18	Access device fraud (10 years in prison) Access device fraud (affecting transactions with unauthorized devices) (15 years in prison)

(1,445 words)

Unit 6

Human Trafficking and Human Smuggling

Part Ⅰ In-class Reading

Pre-reading Questions

- *Could you tell the differences between human smuggling and human trafficking? You can check your answer after reading the following two passages.*
- *Could you collect useful information on how the two countries, the United States and China, control their border?*
- *Could you share your ideas with your partners on the bad effects caused by human trafficking and human smuggling?*

Text A

The International Organization for Migration and People Smuggling

People smuggling is a growing global crime that exposes thousands of migrants to unacceptable risks and challenges the integrity of international borders. In the last two decades, globalization and conflicts have seen an increase in international migration flows. Given the restrictive immigration policies put in place by destination countries and the important human and technological resources deployed at borders to better monitor entry and exit movements, many migrants lacking the means to reach their country destination legally fall prey to criminal groups specialized in people smuggling that can arrange journeys at a high price. The hazardous travel undertaken by these migrants may sometimes be short and direct, but at other times lengthy and circuitous. The time between departure and arrival can vary from a few days to months or even years. Smugglers use land, sea and air routes, but their itineraries can evolve rapidly if detected by border officials. Very often travel conditions are difficult, dangerous and sometimes deadly. At their destination, having crossed an international border illegally, migrants are confronted with their irregular status and usually have very limited means to successfully integrate into their new country's society.

As the leading intergovernmental organization in the field of migration, IOM is increasingly called upon by States to assist in addressing complex border management challenges, including countering people smuggling. The Immigration and Border Management (IBM) Team, consisting of a core group of specialists with substantial technical expertise and strong border management experience, posted to strategic locations in the field as well as in IOM headquarters, has been established to offer guidance and expertise to governments aspiring to improve their migration and border management and operational procedures.

IOM supports States to embed procedures and processes that permit law enforcement agencies to more effectively target those responsible for organising people smuggling while at the same time complementing activity against trafficking in human beings. The IBM Team, for instance, helps governments to identify and source technical equipment required to help detect irregular migrants at border crossings, such as X-ray vehicle scanners or surveillance cameras. The Personal Information and Registration System

(PIRS), IOM's Border Management Information System, can also be a valuable tool to fight smuggling: the system can be connected to national and international alert lists such as Interpol's I-24/7 Global Communication System, and can therefore enable authorities to gather intelligence against organized criminal gangs (movements and routings) and to formulate risk profiles that can assist in identifying both the perpetrators and those being smuggled at an early point in the process. IOM also provides a comprehensive range of training courses designed to equip border officials with the skills necessary to develop and refine intelligence, detect fraudulent travel documents and to be aware of relevant legislation including that related to migrants rights.

Definition of People Smuggling

According to the United Nations Convention on Transnational Organized Crime and its protocol against the smuggling of migrants, people smuggling is "the procurement, in order to obtain, directly or indirectly, a financial or other material benefit, of the illegal entry of a person into a State of which the person is not a national or a permanent resident".

Differentiating Between People Smuggling and Trafficking in Human Beings

People smuggling is distinct from trafficking in human beings insofar as smuggling implies the procurement of irregular entry into a State of which the individual is neither a citizen nor a permanent resident, for financial or material gain. Trafficking, on the other hand, occurs for the purpose of exploitation, often involving forced labour and prostitution. For intermediaries involved in people smuggling, the source of profit derives from the provision of the service of enabling an irregular border crossing, whereas for those involved in organizing human trafficking the source is the exploitation of the person. The difference can also be drawn from the concept of consent. Smuggled individuals are voluntarily involved in the process: they pay people smugglers to enter a country irregularly. Traffickers, on the other hand, use coercion and/or deception to force people into exploitation. Contrary to trafficking, smuggling does not require an element of exploitation, coercion, or violation of human rights. This is not to say that those smuggled are not subject to abuse either before, during or after their journey.

The Western Balkans Smuggling Route

People smugglers are active on routes to the European Union via the external Schengen borders. In 2007, irregular migrants originating in Albania and from third countries were travelling through the dangerously mountainous regions of Kakavije, Kaphistice and elsewhere in Southern Albania to pass the Albanian-Greek border. The migrants using these crossings were mainly Afghan, Albanian, Chinese, Iraqi, Palestinian and Somali. Their destinations were primarily Belgium, France, Italy, Spain and the United Kingdom. Over two months in March and April 2007, Greek Border Police arrested seven people smugglers, detected around 500 forged documents and found almost 450 persons were hidden in cars and vans trying to gain unlawful entry into Greece. Although this route was disrupted as a result, smugglers demonstrated their flexibility and switched to alternative routes via Croatia, Montenegro and Serbia to Italy, Hungary and Slovenia, and then onwards to the West. As a matter of fact, with Albania now benefiting from Schengen visa exemption, criminal groups are increasingly using the Serbian-Hungarian border to smuggle people into the EU: The number of irregular migrants apprehended at this border has raised by 20 percent between January and August 2011 when compared to the same period in 2010. IOM, through its 2009-2011 project "Integrated Border Management in the Western Balkans and Turkey" worked with Albania, Bosnia Herzegovina, Croatia, Kosovo, Macedonia, Montenegro, Serbia and Turkey to build enhanced cooperation in border management and increase officers' skills to counter criminal activities. The specialized Risk Analysis training courses that were delivered in the framework of this project notably addressed the issue of people smuggling. Trainers stressed that the ultimate goal of border management risk analysis was to maximize the effectiveness of controls where the highest risk of criminal activities—including smuggling—was concentrated.

Profitability of Smuggling for Organized Criminal Groups Is Estimated at 3 to 10 Billion USD a Year

For organized crime groups, smuggling people across borders is a "low-risk, high-profit" business. Smugglers still benefit from weak legislation and relatively slim risks of being detected, arrested and prosecuted. Moreover, numerous other crimes are oftentimes linked to people smuggling—human trafficking, identity fraud, corruption and money laundering—creating shadow governance systems that undercut the rule of law. This situation calls for enhanced international cooperation between concerned States' law enforcement agencies, international organizations and other relevant actors.

The Bali Ministerial Conference on People Smuggling, Trafficking in Human Beings and Related Transnational Crime

Following large numbers of illegal boat arrivals run by people smuggling operations in the Asia-Pacific region, the Bali Ministerial Conference on People Smuggling, Trafficking in Persons and Related Transnational Crime was launched in 2002. It brings together more than 40 source, transit and destination countries from throughout the region to combat people smuggling and human trafficking. IOM, together with the UNHCR, Australia, Indonesia, New Zealand and Thailand is part of its steering committee and fosters regional cooperative efforts through technical workshops and increased cooperation between interested countries and agencies such as the International Red Cross and Interpol.

IOM'S border control and migration management assessments

The IBM Team conducts border control and migration management assessments that enable States to identify areas for development and strengthen their immigration and border structures and support the development of operational measures and legal instruments to counter smuggling and related criminal activities. Regional research is also carried out by IOM's country offices to better understand the dynamics behind people smuggling. Publications examples are:

- "In Pursuit of the Southern Dream: Victims of Necessity" highlights the scope and nature of irregular migration and people smuggling of men from East Africa and the Horn to South Africa (2009).
- "Future Tools to Deal with Irregular Migration and Smuggling of Migrants in the European Union" aims at enabling migration management practitioners to better understand the latest developments in Europe (2008).

(1,335 words)

Background Information

▶ IOM

The International Organization for Migration is an intergovernmental organization. It was initially established in 1951 as the Intergovernmental Committee for European Migration (ICEM) to help resettle people displaced by World War Ⅱ. As of December 2013, the International Organization for Migration has 155 member states and 11 observer states.

IOM is the leading inter-governmental organization in the field of migration and works closely with governmental, intergovernmental and non-governmental partners. IOM works to help ensure the orderly and humane management of migration, to promote international cooperation on migration issues, to assist in the search for practical solutions to migration problems and to provide humanitarian assistance to migrants in need, including refugees and internally displaced people.

▶ Schengen Agreement

The Schengen Agreement led to the creation of Europe's borderless Schengen Area in 1995. The treaty was signed on 14 June 1985 between five of the then ten member states of the European Economic Community near the town of Schengen in Luxembourg. The Schengen Agreement abolished internal borders, enabling passport-free movement between a large number of European countries. Schengen is now under review because in 2011 there were surges in illegal migration from Africa and Asia, via Italy and Greece in particular.

▶ The Personal Information and Registration System (PIRS)

The Personal Identification and Registration System (PIRS) is the Border Management Information System developed by the International Organization for Migration (IOM) to support enhanced migration management.

PIRS is a Border Management Information system that allows for the Collection, Processing, Storage, and Dissemination of travelers' information when entering and exiting border points for the purpose of identification, authentication and analysis.

New Words

hazardous [ˈhæzədəs]

adj. Something that is hazardous is dangerous, especially to people's health or safety. 有危害的

E.g. Emergency services described hazardous conditions as they tried to reach people in need of help.

circuitous [səˈkju(ː)ɪtəs]

adj. A circuitous route is long and complicated rather than simple and direct. 迂回的

E.g. After being denied permission to leave China, he quietly crossed the border and came to Germany via a circuitous route.

itinerary [ɑɪˈtɪnərərɪ]

[C] *n.* An itinerary is a plan of a trip, including the route and the places that you will visit. 旅行计划

E.g. The exact itinerary for the American portion of their tour has yet to be released.

embed [ɪmˈbɛd]

vt. 1) If an object embeds itself in a substance or thing, it becomes fixed there firmly and deeply. 嵌入

E.g. It's easy to embed sensors in all sorts of ecosystems, from hospitals to supply chains to natural systems like rivers.

2) If something such as an attitude or feeling is embedded in a society or system, or in someone's personality, it becomes a permanent and noticeable feature of it. 使根深蒂固

E.g. They said a new culture of openness and transparency continued to embed itself within the Northern Ireland Civil Service.

procurement [prəˈkjʊəmənt]

[U] *n.* Procurement is the act of obtaining something such as supplies for an army or other organization. 获得(军需品等的)行为

E.g. Ministers were also committed to tackling waste and corruption in government and public procurement.

prostitution [ˌprɒstɪˈtjuːʃən]

[U] *n.* Prostitution means having sex with people in exchange for money. 卖淫

E.g. Some politicians have called for Botswana to consider legalising prostitution to fight against HIV.

intermediary [ˌɪntəˈmiːdɪərɪ]

[C] *n.* An intermediary is a person who passes messages or proposals between two people or groups. 中间人

E.g. "They're lying," Ashtiani told the Guardian, speaking through the intermediary whom the paper did not name for security reasons.

coercion [kəʊˈɜːʃən]

[U] *n.* Coercion is the act or process of persuading someone forcefully to do something that they do not want to do. 胁迫

E.g. He would not comment further on whether there was evidence of coercion.

forge [fɔːdʒ]

vt. 1) If one person or institution forges an agreement or relationship with another, they create it with a lot of hard work, hoping that it will be strong or lasting. 努力地缔造

E.g. Our goal is to forge a secure and durable peace between Israelis and Palestinians.

2) If someone forges something such as paper money, a document, or a painting, they copy it or make it so that it looks genuine, in order to deceive people. 伪造(纸币、文件或画作等)

E.g. He admitted seven charges including forging passports.

Exercises

▶ Exercise One: Reading comprehension

Answer the following questions in your own words after reading the passage.

1. After reading the passage, please give a brief introduction to the Immigration and Border Management (IBM) Team.
2. What function does the Personal Information and Registration System (PIRS) have when fighting smuggling?

3. What is the definition of people smuggling according to the passage? And what are the differences between people smuggling and trafficking in human beings?

▶ Exercise Two: Translation

Please translate the following sentences into Chinese.

1. Given the restrictive immigration policies put in place by destination countries and the important human and technological resources deployed at borders to better monitor entry and exit movements, many migrants lacking the means to reach their country destination legally fall prey to criminal groups specialized in people smuggling that can arrange journeys at a high price.
2. The Immigration and Border Management (IBM) Team, consisting of a core group of specialists with substantial technical expertise and strong border management experience, posted to strategic locations in the field as well as in IOM headquarters, has been established to offer guidance and expertise to governments aspiring to improve their migration and border management and operational procedures.
3. IOM supports States to embed procedures and processes that permit law enforcement agencies to more effectively target those responsible for organising people smuggling while at the same time complementing activity against trafficking in human beings.
4. The IBM Team conducts border control and migration management assessments that enable States to identify areas for development and strengthen their immigration and border structures and support the development of operational measures and legal instruments to counter smuggling and related criminal activities.

Part Ⅱ After-class Reading

Text B

International Cooperation in Trafficking in Persons Cases

International cooperation in criminal matters is an essential prerequisite to combat trafficking in persons. A significant proportion of trafficking in persons cases are transnational and even those cases within a single jurisdiction may involve victims or offenders who originate outside that jurisdiction. A given set of facts may justify and give rise to criminal investigations and prosecutions in multiple jurisdictions. Informal and formal methods of international cooperation are important in order to deprive traffickers' safe haven.

International cooperation in criminal matters can be very challenging and requires knowledge, planning and awareness of practical issues at stake in both the requested and the requesting States. Some of these issues include but are not limited to the cost of investigations, the venue of trial, the applicable legal framework, nationality, the location of witnesses, the location of offenders, gathering of evidence and admissibility of evidence rules. However, with a little experience, the benefits of using tools of international cooperation will greatly outweigh these challenges.

Different forms of international cooperation include, among others:

- Extradition,
- Mutual legal assistance,
- Transfer of criminal proceedings,
- Transfer of sentenced persons,
- Cooperation for purposes of confiscation to deprive traffickers of

criminal assets,

- Cooperation between law enforcement authorities including exchanging information and cooperation in conducting inquiries,
- Joint investigations, and
- Cooperation in using special investigative techniques.

Channels of communication of international cooperation include (who is contacted will depend on the type of cooperation needed, legal requirements of the requested state and the provisions of the agreement in issue):

- Competent national authorities or central authorities,
- Diplomatic staff, and
- Law enforcement officials.

It should be noted that the forms of cooperation mentioned above could complement each other with a view to ensuring that the widest measure of assistance is afforded in investigations, prosecutions and judicial proceedings related to trafficking in persons.

Examples of more structured forms of cooperation in law enforcement include:

- Posting liaison officers to facilitate cooperation with the host government's law enforcement officers in criminal investigations,
- Bilateral and multilateral agreements and arrangements on law enforcement cooperation and on the sharing of law enforcement information, and
- Cooperation within such structures as the International Criminal Police Organization (INTERPOL), or various regional cooperation structures such as the European Police Office (Europol) or Eurojust.

Judicial cooperation in criminal matters provides a more formal framework for cooperation compared with the cooperation in law enforcement. The tools available are based on bilateral and multilateral agreements and arrangements or, in some cases and in the absence of such agreements and arrangements, directly on national law.

Both informal and formal law enforcement cooperation, however, have been hampered by a number of problems, such as:

- Diversity of legal systems,
- Diversity of law enforcement structures,
- Absence of channels of communication for the exchange, for example, of basic information and criminal intelligence,
- Diversity in approaches and priorities, and
- Lack of trust.

Case Example 1

In some jurisdictions the police have considerable autonomy, directing and conducting enquiries. Within such a system there may be a culture of very informal officer-to-officer contact. Prosecutors and courts accept such informal contact. For instance, in Re Sealed's case, the United States Court of Appeals rejected the argument that Untied States law enforcement agencies were limited to obtaining evidence in accordance with the provisions set out in the mutual legal assistance treaty signed by the Swiss and United States Governments. In other systems the police may be directed by investigating prosecutors or magistrates and such direct informal contact would not be acceptable. Misunderstandings can arise if those working under one system do not understand the other system.

The United Nations Convention Against Transnational Organized Crime (UNTOC) contains detailed provisions on both formal and informal cooperation in criminal matters, which are also applicable, mutatis mutandis, to the Trafficking Protocol, as follows:

- Extradition,
- Transfer of sentenced persons,
- Mutual legal assistance,
- Joint investigations,

- Cooperation in using special investigative techniques,
- Transfer of criminal proceedings,
- International cooperation for purposes of confiscation, and
- Law enforcement cooperation.

In general terms, States parties can use UNTOC as a legal basis for international cooperation.

In the field of extradition, States parties that make extradition conditional on the existence of a treaty are required to inform the Secretary-General whether they will consider the Convention as the legal basis for this form of cooperation. States may also use national legislation and/or the principle of reciprocity to execute extradition requests.

In the field of mutual legal assistance, article 18 includes a set of provisions that can be used by countries not bound by relevant bilateral treaties or by States that have already concluded such treaties and may wish to complement them.

Case example 2

A case investigated in Bulgaria involved extensive cooperation with the Netherlands. The Dutch prosecutor contacted the International Legal Assistance department of the Supreme Cassation Prosecutors Office in Sofia to establish which colleague was working on the case in question in Bulgaria. The Dutch prosecutor then made direct contact with his counterpart in Bulgaria.

The Netherlands then sent a letter of request to the Bulgarian court requesting that some items of evidence (money and jewellery) be frozen and seized as part of the investigation. The Bulgarian court gave its permission and the items were seized by the Bulgarian public prosecution and sent as evidence to the Netherlands. Once the Dutch authorities reached a final decision on the case, the seized items were returned to Bulgaria and became confiscated items of the Bulgarian state.

Furthermore, the Dutch requested that their authorities were present during the taping of telephone conversations intercepted in Bulgaria. They made this request to ensure that evidence gathered was in accordance with Dutch evidentiary procedures and therefore were admissible in the Dutch court.

(952 words)

Unit 7

International Police Cooperation

Part Ⅰ In-class Reading

Pre-reading Questions

- *What role does the international police cooperation play when combating the transnational crime? Why?*
- *What aspects do you think the international police cooperation should consist of?*
- *What can the law enforcement agencies around the world do to make sure that the international police cooperation goes smoothly?*

Text A

The Types of International Police Cooperation

The intensity of international law enforcement cooperation has greatly accelerated in recent years. The types of cooperation introduced to combat the increasing problems posed by transborder or international criminality can be classified as bilateral, global, and regional.

Bilateral Cooperation

This is the oldest and remains, in some respects, the most important type of police cooperation. Although often based on informal understandings, bilateral police treaties first appeared in the nineteenth century and have become increasingly common in the last twenty-five years. These seldom give an accurate impression of the significance and the value of this cooperation. The scope of the agreements, as the model agreement prepared by INTERPOL in 1975 illustrates, is potentially very wide. They can cover the exchange of general police information concerning matters such as traffic accidents, missing or stolen property, the exchange of crime prevention information about the operating methods of criminals, people in need of protection, the surveillance of suspects, and the reporting of the transport of dangerous substances.

Cooperation in criminal investigations can consist of the exchange of information or evidence, exchange of police investigation records, police officers on mission, and hot pursuit of offenders across international borders. Agreements can also include the naming of police authorities competent to engage in transborder cooperation, the location and frequency of international meetings, methods of communication between the cooperating police forces, the role of the National Central Bureaus of INTERPOL, requests to enter the territory of another state, regulations concerning the use of vehicles and the carrying of firearms, and civil liabilities of police in foreign countries. In practice, police treaties or agreements never include all of these items. Agreements may also take the form of semi-confidential protocols or the exchange of letters of understanding. One type of agreement is virtually universal among neighboring friendly countries—the arrangements for policing land frontiers. Recently in Europe, these have been developed to include joint police stations, which can be important points of contact and coordination.

Another form of police cooperation is the exchange or the posting of police liaison officers in foreign countries. After World War Ⅱ, the United States pioneered the practice of having law enforcement officers as embassy attaches. The large number of federal law enforcement agencies led to a proliferation of police officers on overseas postings: Members of the FBI, the DEA (Drug Enforcement Administration), U.S. Customs, the Internal Revenue Service, the Secret Service, and the Immigration and Naturalization Service can be found in some key embassies. This law enforcement presence is sometimes a sensitive political matter in host countries; the entrepreneurial style of activities of some U.S. law enforcement officials can be viewed as constituting an infringement of sovereignty.

The FBI is the first one to establish overseas representation in the aftermath of World War Ⅱ through legats (legal attaches) in major embassies for the purposes of counter-intelligence and in the fight against international organized crime, including terrorism. The DEA, which has maintained up to sixty permanent offices in forty-three countries, has more personnel overseas than does the FBI. The DEA and its supporters believe that intelligence gathering, in source and transit countries, reduces the importation of drugs into the United States. The more flamboyant Latin American operations of the DEA have included the arrest of drug traffickers in foreign jurisdictions and bringing them to the United States for trial, and joint operations with police and military in Latin American countries to destroy drug crops. The other two federal agencies, U.S. Customs and the Secret Service, prominently involved in international affairs, have much less extensive overseas presence.

The practice of police liaison officers in foreign postings has spread from the United States to countries as far apart as Canada, Japan, and Israel. In Europe, the French Technical Service for International Police Cooperation (the SCTIP) has, since the 1960s, developed an impressive international network for advising on police techniques, equipment, and training. In 1971 the Franco-American agreement on arrangements to combat the "French connection" (the flow of Turkish opium, which is refined into heroin in the Marseilles area for onward shipment to the United States) included the exchange of liaison officers, and in 1986 it was extended to include Canada and Italy. In the 1980s, drug liaison officers were also sent out from various European countries to drug producing and transit countries. Since the mid-1980s, liaison officers specializing in terrorism have been exchanged among France, Italy, and Germany. The number of liaison officers has subsequently grown, and increasingly they have become generalists rather than specialists.

The liaison officer system has advantages because it allows direct personal contact among law enforcement officers in different countries. This can expedite investigations, particularly by putting investigating officers in touch with the right authorities in the cooperating country. The good liaison officer can be a valuable resource in helping to clear up misunderstandings, and provide information about a foreign jurisdiction and its criminal investigation policies. Sending police officers on a temporary mission for particular inquiries or missions is not usually regarded as an adequate substitute for liaison officers, because often the former cannot acquire sufficient information about the country in a short time.

Global Cooperation

INTERPOL is the key agency for global law enforcement cooperation, but the United Nations, the Customs Cooperation Council, the G8 (Group of the world's most highly industrialized nations), and the Organization for Economic Co-operation and Development also play important, if intermittent, roles in promoting cooperation. INTERPOL provides a system of multilateral communication of police information; it helps coordinate inquiries and its secretary general can initiate them.

The origins of INTERPOL are curious and its international status uncertain—some observers feel that the lack of a treaty basis for the organization detracts from its authority and legitimacy. But the organization is now almost universally accepted as an intergovernmental organization and has received important support from the United States. It has radically upgraded its computer and communications equipment, become more open with the media, dropped its practice of non-involvement in terrorist cases, and has generally become more adaptable in the face of changing patterns of international crime. Although its reputation varies in the law enforcement community over time and according to region of the world, it is an indispensable communications system and an important link between national police forces.

The United Nations plays an essential supportive role in international law enforcement—as a forum in which international treaties can be negotiated (on subjects such as trafficking in people, crime prevention, and human rights), a repository for statistical and legal information about criminal matters, and provider of aid to improve the capacity for criminal law enforcement in less developed countries. Its biggest influence on practical law enforcement has been in the field of drug trafficking. The work of the United Nations' Division of Narcotic Drugs (UNDND), established shortly after the founding of the UN, has since January 1992 amalgamated with other antidrug activities of the UN International Drug Control Program (UNIDCP) and promoted four basic conventions: the 1961 Convention on Narcotic Drugs, the 1971 Convention on Psychotropic Drugs, the 1988 Vienna Convention (mainly concerned with law enforcement measures), and the 1999 Convention on Organized Crime.

The harmonization of efforts in drug law enforcement and the repression of financial crime has been supported by the action of the Group of Eight (now known as G8, which holds periodic meetings), through measures against money laundering, including the setting up of a Financial Action

Task Force (FATF) in the Organization for Economic Cooperation and Development (OECD) and encouraging the setting up of national financial intelligence units. These latter members of an international network known as the Egmont Group, act as clearinghouses for information and are national points of contact.

Regional Cooperation

In the Americas there is much law enforcement interaction on a multilateral basis through the regional meetings of INTERPOL, the International Drug Enforcement Conference, the Organization of American States, and the International Association of Chiefs of Police, but very little of this directly involves police operations. Operational cooperation is almost entirely on a bilateral basis, and most of it is initiated by the United States. Apart from interesting developments within the Association of South East Asian Nations, this applies also to other continents. The exception is Western Europe, where there have been moves toward institutionalized forms of law enforcement cooperation during the last two decades.

The most intensive regional cooperation is now taking place in the European Union. This started with the Trevi Group—the regular meeting of the Ministries of Justice and the Interior of the EC countries set up in 1975 to coordinate measures against terrorism but whose remit was widened to include other forms of serious crime, and exchanges about police techniques, training, and equipment. The 1991 Maastricht Treaty gave a legal basis to Europol, specifically to developments in the fields of coordination of investigation and search procedures; the creation of databases; the analysis of criminal intelligence on a Europe-wide basis; joint crime prevention strategies; and measures relating to further training, research, forensic matters, and criminal records departments. Europol, based in The Hague, became fully operational in 1996.

The two Schengen Agreements (1985 and 1990) "compensate" for the abolition of border checks on goods and persons between EU member states, and contain measures for operational police cooperation. All members of the European Union are members of Schengen, although Britain, Ireland, and Denmark have partial opt-outs. The Schengen system provides the instruments that are needed for policing the external frontiers (that is, frontiers with non-EU countries) and for quick responses to any law enforcement problem between member countries. The first objective is to be achieved mainly by means of an online database, the Schengen Information System (SIS, now SIS Ⅱ), containing information such as wanted persons or persons in need of protection, prohibited immigrants, and stolen or suspected vehicles. The second objective is sought through an emergency operations system called the SIRENE. In SIRENE, national offices review requests for immediate operational action, with a check on the legality of the action requested and forward it to the appropriate police authority.

The EU law enforcement agenda moved on decisively under the influence of two developments. First, in 1999 the EU adopted the Tampere program, which envisaged development of more integrated operational police cooperation in order to confront shared law enforcement problems. Second, the terrorist events of September 11, 2001, in the United States gave a political impetus to this program and resulted in the European Arrest Warrant (which replaces the cumbersome extradition proceedings), cross-border freezing of assets, rapid procedures for the transfer of evidence, joint investigation teams, better cooperation between prosecution services, upgrading of Europol's anti-terrorist unit, and enhanced cooperation with U.S. law enforcement agencies.

(1,774 words)

Background Information

▶ DEA

The Drug Enforcement Administration (DEA) is a United States federal law enforcement agency under the U.S. Department of Justice, tasked with combating drug smuggling and use within the United States. The mission of the DEA is to enforce the controlled substances laws and regulations of the United States and bring to the criminal and civil justice system of the United States, or any other competent jurisdiction, those organizations and principal members of organizations, involved in the growing, manufacture, or distribution of controlled substances appearing in or destined for illicit traffic in the United States; and to recommend and support non-enforcement programs aimed at reducing the availability of illicit controlled substances on the domestic and international markets.

Not only is the DEA the lead agency for domestic enforcement of the Controlled Substances Act, sharing concurrent jurisdiction with the Federal Bureau of Investigation (FBI) and Immigration and Customs Enforcement (ICE), it also has sole responsibility for coordinating and pursuing U.S. drug investigations abroad.

▶ G8

The Group of Eight (G8) was the name of a forum for the governments of a group of eight leading industrialised countries that was originally formed by six leading industrialised countries (France, the United States, Britain, Germany, Japan and Italy) and subsequently extended with two additional members (Canada and Russia).

Russia, which was invited to join as the last member, was excluded from the forum by the other members on March 24, 2014, as a result of its involvement in the 2014 Crimea crisis in Ukraine. Thus the group now comprises seven nations and will continue to meet as the G7 group of nations.

New Words

liability [ˌlaɪəˈbɪlɪtɪ]

[C] *n.* 1) If you say that someone or something is a liability, you mean that they cause a lot of problems or embarrassment. 累赘

E.g. As the money she made continues to fall, they're clearly beginning to consider her a liability.

2) A company's or organization's liabilities are the sums of money which it owes. [商]负债

E.g. The company is reported to have liabilities of nearly $90,000.

confidential [ˌkɒnfɪˈdɛnʃəl]

adj. 1) Information that is confidential is meant to be kept secret or private. 保密的

E.g. Obviously the details of our agreement with Sheffield United will, and should, remain confidential.

2) If you talk to someone in a confidential way, you talk to them quietly because what you are saying is secret or private. 悄悄的

E.g. She told me confidentially that she is going to retire early.

frontier [ˈfrʌntiə]

[C] *n.* 1) A frontier is a border between two countries. 国界

E.g. With the strict border management, it is difficult then to cross the frontier.

2) The frontiers of something, especially knowledge, are the limits to which it extends. (尤指知识的)前沿

E.g. ... pushing back the frontiers of science.

embassy [ˈɛmbəsɪ]

[C] *n.* An embassy is a group of government officials, headed by an ambassador, who represent their government in a foreign country. The building in which they work is also called an embassy. 大使及其随

员;大使馆

E.g. Security concerns also prompted Jordan to shut down its embassy established before the Iraq war.

entrepreneurial [ˌɒntrəprəˈnɜːriəl]

adj. Entrepreneurial means having the qualities that are needed to succeed as an entrepreneur. [商]具有创业素质的

E.g. Big corporations usually bring much needed business expertise and entrepreneurial skills to developing countries.

infringement [ɪnˈfrɪndʒmənt]

[C] *n.* 1) An infringement is an action or situation that interferes with your rights and the freedom you are entitled to. (对他人权利或自由等的)侵犯

E.g. Nokia has extended its legal action against Apple by filing 13 more patent infringement claims.

2) An infringement of a law or rule is the act of breaking it or disobeying it. 违反

E.g. Undoubtedly, there have been an infringement of the rules in the organization.

flamboyant [flæmˈbɔɪənt]

adj. If you say that someone or something is flamboyant, you mean that they are very noticeable, stylish, and exciting. 耀眼的;派头十足的

E.g. He was flamboyant and temperamental on and off the stage.

expedite [ˈɛkspɪˌdaɪt]

vt. (formal) to make a process happen more quickly 加快

E.g. We have developed rapid order processing to expedite deliveries to customers.

intermittent [ˌɪntəˈmɪtənt]

adj. Something that is intermittent happens occasionally rather than continuously. 断断续续的

E.g. Over the next few years, he could only find intermittent work on and off.

detract [dɪˈtrækt]

vt./vi. If one thing detracts from another, it makes it seem less good or impressive. 减损

E.g. Nothing that comes after will be able to detract from the importance of this first great step forward.

repository [rɪˈpɒzɪtərɪ]

[C] *n.* A repository is a place where something is kept safely. [正式]贮存处；存放处

E.g. The office became a repository for police files.

psychotropic [ˌsaɪkəʊˈtrɒpɪk]

adj. Psychotropic drugs are drugs that affect your mind. (药物)作用于精神的

E.g. Among psychotropic medications, two classes are particularly effective for panic, and they are very different from each other.

clearinghouse [ˈklɪəɪŋhaʊs]

[C] *n.* 1) If an organization acts as a clearinghouse, it collects, sorts, and distributes specialized information. 专门信息搜集所

E.g. The foundation serves as a clearinghouse for information about the nation's health care system.

2) A clearinghouse is a central bank which deals with all business among the banks that use its services. [商](银行之间的)结算所

remit [rɪˈmɪt]

n. the area of activity over which a particular person or group has authority, control or influence 职责之内,控制范围,影响范围等

E.g. Such decisions are outside the remit of this committee.

vt. 1) to send money, etc. to a person or place 汇钱

E.g. Payment will be remitted to you in full.

2) to cancel or free sb. from a debt, duty, punishment, etc. 免除

E.g. Based on the evidence, the judge decided to remit a prison sentence for him.

envisage [ɪnˈvɪzɪdʒ]

vt. If you envisage something, you imagine that it is true, real, or likely to happen. 设想

E.g. He said he did not envisage any changes to the present system.

Exercises

▶ Exercise One: Reading comprehension

Answer the following questions in your own words after reading the passage.

1. How many types can international police cooperation be divided into? And what are these types?
2. What are the two forms of the bilateral police cooperation?
3. Which agency is the most important one for global law enforcement cooperation? What does the key agency provide for global police cooperation?
4. Where is the most intensive regional cooperation now taking place?

▶ Exercise Two: Translation

Please translate the following sentences into Chinese.

1. They (Agreements) can cover the exchange of general police information concerning matters such as traffic accidents, missing or stolen property, the exchange of crime prevention information about the operating methods of criminals, people in need of protection, the surveillance of suspects, and the reporting of the transport of dangerous substances.
2. The United Nations plays an essential supportive role in international law enforcement—as a forum in which international treaties can be negotiated (on subjects such as trafficking in people, crime prevention, and human rights), a

repository for statistical and legal information about criminal matters, and provider of aid to improve the capacity for criminal law enforcement in less developed countries.

3. The harmonization of efforts in drug law enforcement and the repression of financial crime has been supported by the action of the Group of Eight (now known as G8, which holds periodic meetings), through measures against money laundering, including the setting up of a Financial Action Task Force (FATF) in the Organization for Economic Cooperation and Development (OECD) and encouraging the setting up of national financial intelligence units.
4. The most intensive regional cooperation is now taking place in the European Union. This started with the Trevi Group—the regular meeting of the Ministries of Justice and the Interior of the EC countries set up in 1975 to coordinate measures against terrorism but whose remit was widened to include other forms of serious crime, and exchanges about police techniques, training, and equipment.

Part Ⅱ After-class Reading

Text B

The Need for International Police Cooperation

An Increasing Threat of Transnational Crime

The propensity of criminals to cross national borders—to engage in "transnational crime"—is certainly not a new phenomenon; it is probably as old as the borders themselves. Borders were established to delineate the jurisdiction claimed by each state, and crossing national borders has often provided criminals with a way to mitigate or avoid the consequences of illegal acts. Yet in spite of a long, eventful history, there is strong evidence that transnational crime has become more prevalent and serious today than ever before.

Our Shrinking World

We live in a different world from that of our parents and grandparents, and many of the differences facilitate greater transnational crime. Consider, for example, the following five developments, all within the last twenty-five years: (1) Transportation systems have improved and expanded dramatically, particularly airline and automobile travel; international tourism and business travel are at record levels. (2) Communication systems have improved and expanded most notably satellite and fiber optic telephone and television transmission, FAX transmission, and computer information storage, processing, and transmission. (3) The breakup of the Soviet Union has reduced or eliminated many trade and travel restrictions between East and West, reduced the level of social control within and between many of the former Soviet Block countries, and made obsolete many countries' Cold War fears and policies. (4) World trade has expanded, including stronger participation by the economies of Eastern Europe, Asia, the Middle East, and the "Third World"; world economic interdependence is now a basic fact of life. (5) Perhaps most significant of all, the world's population has increased, resulting in more crowding, more areas of poverty, disease, and hunger, and large movements of people across national borders. The cumulative effect of these conditions is more people, more opportunities and possibly reasons for committing crime, and more effective movement of people and information across national borders—a perfect setup for increased transnational crime. It is no wonder that our newspapers now regularly report incidences of international terrorism, theft, smuggling, securities and currency violations, computer crimes, fleeing from justice, drug trafficking, and illegal immigration—just to name a few.

The Police Mission

A distinguishing feature of modern civilization is the use of governmental institutions—police, courts, and correctional agencies—to intervene on society's behalf to resolve conflicts and enforce basic social rules. Such "state" justice, properly administered, is deemed superior to the earlier private "justice" that featured physical, often brutal and unrestrained, conflict between individuals, families, or tribes. A primary goal of state justice is to control social violence and destruction, and to protect the weak from victimization; however, if governments today, primarily through their police agencies, and to effectively protect citizens from crime and enforce society's rules, they must increasingly be able to deal with crime that is transnational in nature.

A second primary goal of state justice, is the serving of each society's own dominant values and customs in the administration of "justice". Hence, each society has its own enforcement style and priorities, and even some of its own laws—factors that complicate and occasionally frustrate attempts at international police cooperation.

Overcoming the Limits of Jurisdiction

Transnational crime, by definition, involves two or more countries, each claiming sovereignty and exclusive criminal jurisdiction within its own borders. Hence, when a criminal crosses the border, any pursuing police officers "lose" their jurisdiction. To overcome this problem, governments and their police agencies have employed numerous strategies. Some involve direct, unilateral, extralegal police action within another country or official collusion to circumvent the law, and some involve cooperative, bilateral, legally-sanctioned actions by one country's police, or by a multinational police task force, on behalf of another country. The first of these two "kinds" of strategies is predicated on violating international law and other countries' sovereignty; the second is based on legality and cooperation.

Guiding Principles for Improvement

Given our experiences to date in policing transnational crime, two principles immediately suggest themselves for guiding our attempts to do better in the future. First, we should found our international police working relationships on properly negotiated agreements—that is, on mutual respect, benefit, and consent—rather than political or economic coercion, violation of foreign sovereignty, or extralegal collusion. Second, related to the first, is the achievement of greater consistency, effectiveness, predictability, and legitimacy in the relationships. These principles are admittedly idealistic and difficult to achieve, but they are worth keeping in mind and worth working for.

Specific Needs for Cooperation

From a practical police perspective, certain specific acts of international cooperation are regularly needed to deal with transnational crime. Initially, there is a need for discovering, documenting, and communicating basic working information about crimes, for example: What happened? When? Where? Description of suspects? Injuries? Next, there is a need for direct acts of investigative assistance, for example, locating and arresting suspects, collecting evidence, identifying and interviewing witnesses, and detaining and extraditing suspects. Finally, there is frequently a need for help in prosecution, for example, deposing witnesses or arranging for their appearance in court, having investigative personnel testify in court, and if a conviction occurs, providing the sentencing judge with background information about the suspect to guide the determination of an appropriate punishment.

Other forms of transnational police cooperation, less commonly recognized but potentially as important, include the sharing of law enforcement expertise, technology, and resources, the exchange of cultural information and philosophy, and the sharing of "off duty" social and recreational activities. These latter forms of cooperation offer potential benefits far beyond facilitating law enforcement's capacity to control crime.

(920 words)

Unit 8

Interpol

Part Ⅰ In-class Reading

Pre-reading Questions

- *Please collect more information about INTERPOL and get your own understanding on what factors make INTERPOL a quite successful police organization in the world.*
- *In the war against the international crimes, what benefits does Interpol I-24/7 bring to the success? Give the supporting examples.*

Text A

Interpol I-24/7

Eighty years ago, Interpol was created to develop ways of improving communication between national police services in order to detect and prevent international crime and terrorism. This job is more difficult today, due in part to the ease of international travel, revolutionary changes in forms of communication, and the creation of scores of new nations. The importance of effective international police communication has never been more evident or more challenging.

To meet this challenge, in 2002 Interpol Secretary General Ronald K. Noble launched a state-of-the-art communication system to connect the Interpol membership of more than 180 countries and to replace the former, ageing system. One hundred countries have already connected to the new system.

Interpol's new internet-based global police communication system is called I-24/7. I-24/7 stands for Interpol, twenty four hours a day, seven days a week and is intended to help put Interpol's member countries at the forefront of effective international crime fighting.

I-24/7 provides Interpol member countries with immediate, user-friendly access to vital police information in a way which could not previously be contemplated. In addition to giving an instant and effective international messaging capability, I-24/7 provides direct access to an international database of international criminals. It also provides instant access to the Interpol website which contains a range of crime-related information for law enforcement use.

Whilst I-24/7 is barely a year old, it has already made an impact on the way police communicate and collaborate. Interpol member countries regularly inform the General Secretariat in Lyon about ways in which the new system has assisted them in their investigations and, in many instances, made the case. Some examples:

An international drugs trafficker wanted by countries in the Americas and Europe was jailed in Brazil after he was identified at a border control where access to I-24/7 revealed that he was a fugitive offender. Had it not been for the critical services provided through I-24/7, this international criminal might still be on the loose today. Another international criminal was arrested in Porto Seguro while travelling on a false passport.

The I-24/7 messaging facility permitted the instantaneous and secure exchange of photographs, fingerprints, and copies of the fraudulent passport between the member countries involved. Within hours, I-24/7 revealed the true identity of this individual as a renowned international drugs trafficker.

The following incident was reported by Hong Kong, China, whereby I-24/7 played a key role in the arrest of a fugitive wanted by the authorities. An Interpol notice was published at the request of Hong Kong in relation to a theft. The Interpol office in Canberra immediately issued an alert that this person had just left Australia on a flight to Santiago, via Auckland and Buenos Aires. Quick and secure exchanges through I-24/7 enabled each country involved to monitor the fugitive's movements and a formal request for his arrest and surrender was sent to Canberra. This led to his arrest shortly after his arrival at the Sydney Kingsford Smith International Airport. It is unlikely that this arrest would have been possible without the use of the new I-24/7 system where the ability to share time-sensitive information between police services throughout the world was critical.

By connecting national law enforcement agencies to I-24/7 beyond the Interpol National Central Bureaus, member countries are providing their police with the tools to target international criminals where they are often at their most vulnerable (borders, airports, seaports and transit points). What could be more useful for border control officials than to have hands-on access to critical information when unsuspecting criminals present themselves for passport inspection? What could be a more daunting prospect to runaway felons than to have their criminal history available to national police within seconds in every country to which they flee?

Interpol Brazil has connected many of its national law enforcement entities to the system, particularly border controls at international airports and transit points. This has optimized the work performed by its regional offices which can now query Interpol databases directly and take immediate action where necessary.

Similarly, Argentina has expanded its I-24/7 connection to international transit points, particularly its airports and seaports. I-24/7 is now providing permanent police assistance and critical information at the Ezeiza International Airport in Buenos Aires, the Jorge Newbery Airport, the Buenos Aires seaport, and its international central bus station. Of particular significance is the connection of I-24/7 at Puerto Iguazu International Airport, a strategic border point given its triple frontier with Argentina, Paraguay, and Brazil. Other countries, including Germany, the UK, and Canada, have also extended their I-24/7 access beyond the NCBs.

Security is a primary consideration for the safe implementation and operation of the new Interpol global communications system. The messages and databases must be protected as they contain confidential police information. The architecture includes security through maximum level encryption over a virtual private network (VPN). Using the highest levels of encryption, firewalls, a sophisticated password access system, and constantly updated anti-virus software, the security of the new system is of paramount importance and will constantly be tested and upgraded as technology develops.

Security is not, however, exclusively a technological issue. It is also ensured through a controlled process of granting or denying access to the network, in addition to determining and monitoring the kind of access for individual end-users. An Interpol I-24/7 security charter has been adopted to ensure that NCBs are fully aware of and implement their responsibilities in terms of safeguarding network security.

But I-24/7 is more than just a telecommunications system. The ability to search different databases via a single gateway increases the chances of connecting vital pieces of information and, therefore, improving police work and effectiveness. I-24/7 puts essential and accurate information in the right place at the right time, resulting in police officers and other law enforcement officials having the ability to act quickly and decisively.

It is in the interests of national and international security that all Interpol's member countries are connected to I-24/7 as quickly as possible. Strong support from Governments and senior police officials is required to connect the remaining member countries, and to ensure countries fully understand the full impact I-24/7 can have on national security. National support and commitment is also required to ensure all countries recognise the importance of connecting I-24/7 beyond the Interpol offices to national boundaries and transit points (borders, airports, seaports, etc.). Interpol has received financial and technical support for this unique project. This support is vital not only to Interpol and the countries concerned, but to all of us, as this system will encourage immeasurably improved police co-operation in the fight against international crime and terrorism.

(1,098 words)

Background Information

▸ Interpol National Central Bureau

At the heart of every INTERPOL member country is a National Central Bureau (NCB), linking national police with our global network. It is typically a division of the national police agency or investigation service and serves as the contact point for all INTERPOL activities in the field.

Staffed by highly trained police officers, NCBs are the lifeblood of INTERPOL, contributing to our criminal databases and cooperating together on cross-border investigations, operations and arrests.

Given the cross-border nature of organized crime, NCBs work together increasingly on a regional basis. In all regions of the world, we see our member countries combining resources and expertise in successful interventions against those crime areas that affect them the most — from tackling counterfeit and pirated goods in South America, to illegal soccer gambling in Asia and ivory trafficking in Africa.

In the past decade, NCBs have become more active in shaping INTERPOL's activities and plans. The Heads of NCB Conference, initiated in 2005, provides a unique forum for building relationships, sharing information and working together to find joint solutions to common challenges.

▶ Virtual Private Network(VPN)

A virtual private network (VPN) extends a private network across a public network, such as the Internet. It enables a computer to send and receive data across shared or public networks as if it is directly connected to the private network, while benefiting from the functionality, security and management policies of the private network. A VPN is created by establishing a virtual point-to-point connection through the use of dedicated connections, virtual tunneling protocols, or traffic encryptions.

New Words

contemplate [ˈkɒntɛmˌpleɪt]

vt. 1) If you contemplate an action, you think about whether to do it or not. 考虑

E.g. You're too young to be contemplating retirement.

2) If you contemplate an idea or subject, you think about it carefully for a long time. 对……考虑再三

E.g. I can't contemplate what it would be like to be alone.

3) If you contemplate something or someone, you look at them for a long time. 凝视

E.g. She contemplated him in silence.

collaborate [kəˈlæbəˌreɪt]

vi. 1) When one person or group collaborates with another, they work together, especially on a book or on some research.（尤指著书或进行研究时的）合作

E.g. The two hospitals have collaborated on many projects over the years.

2) If someone collaborates with an enemy that is occupying their country during a war, they help them. 通敌

E.g. He was accused of collaborating with the enemy.

fugitive [ˈfjuːdʒɪtɪv]

[C] *n.* A fugitive is someone who is running away or hiding, usually in order to avoid being caught by the police.（通常为避免被警察抓住的）逃避者

E.g. Law enforcement officials won't discuss the case because the perpetrator remains a fugitive.

instantaneous [ˌɪnstənˈteɪnɪəs]

adj. Something that is instantaneous happens immediately and very quickly. 即刻的

E.g. Of course Twitter isn't the only medium whose instantaneous nature can prove extremely dangerous.

daunting [ˈdɔːntɪŋ]

adj. Something that is daunting makes you feel slightly afraid or worried about dealing with it. 使人畏缩的

E.g. The country's recent general election may have thrown up an array of daunting challenges.

felon [ˈfɛlən]

[C] *n.* A felon is a person who is guilty of committing a felony. [法]重罪犯

E.g. Jabaar Vincent Thomas, 26, of Los Angeles was charged with three counts of second-degree robbery and one count of being a felon in possession of a handgun.

encrypt [ɪnˈkrɪpt]

vt. If a document or piece of information is encrypted, it is written in a special code, so that only certain people can read it. 把……译成密码;加密

E.g. Account details are encrypted to protect privacy.

账户信息均加以密码,以保护隐私。

→派生词 encryption [U] *n.*

E.g. It is currently illegal to export this encryption technology to other countries.

firewall [ˈfaɪəwɔːl]

[C] *n.* A firewall is a computer system or program that automatically prevents an unauthorized person from gaining access to a computer when it is connected to a network such as the Internet. (网络)防火墙

E.g. Like the firewall, running multiple anti-virus suites can cause software conflicts and create major computer performance issues.

Exercises

▶ Exercise One: Reading comprehension

Answer the following questions in your own words after reading the passage.

1. What does I-24/7, Interpol's new internet-based global police communication system stand for?
2. What can I-24/7 provide for Interpol member countries?
3. What does Interpol do to safeguard the security of I-24/7?

▶ Exercise Two: Translation

Please translate the following sentences into Chinese.

1. By connecting national law enforcement agencies to I-24/7 beyond the Interpol National Central Bureaus, member countries are providing their police with the tools to target international criminals where they are often at their most vulnerable (borders, airports, sea-ports and transit points).

2. What could be more useful for border control officials than to have hands-on access to critical information when unsuspecting criminals present themselves for passport inspection? What could be a more daunting prospect to runaway felons than to have their criminal history available to national police within seconds in every country to which they flee?
3. Using the highest levels of encryption, firewalls, a sophisticated password access system, and constantly updated anti-virus software, the security of the new system is of paramount importance and will constantly be tested and upgraded as technology develops.
4. The ability to search different databases via a single gateway increases the chances of connecting vital pieces of information and, therefore, improving police work and effectiveness. I-24/7 puts essential and accurate information in the right place at the right time, resulting in police officers and other law enforcement officials having the ability to act quickly and decisively.

Part Ⅱ After-class Reading

Text B

Integrated Solutions to Access INTERPOL's Databases—MIND and FIND

Interpol is offering countries the opportunity to give their frontline officers instant access to its many databases. These databases contain millions of records of criminal information on individuals and property submitted by member countries, constituting a unique and vast collection of data that does not exist at the regional or national levels.

INTERPOL manages a database of passports, identity cards and visas reported as stolen or lost by countries all over the world known as the stolen and lost travel documents (SLTD) database. It enables frontline officers to check instantly whether a travel document is stolen or lost. INTERPOL also has databases on stolen motor vehicles and wanted persons.

There are millions of stolen or lost travel documents in circulation today. How can an immigration officer at an airport, seaport or land border crossing know if a passport is stolen or not? What are the consequences for national security if a terrorist or criminal enters a country using a stolen travel document and false identity?

At field level, most countries rely on their own national sources of information. Yet crime is increasingly globalized. Real-time access to up-to-date international information is vital to prevent criminals from traveling freely to escape from the law or commit further crimes.

To help countries connect easily, INTERPOL has developed two integrated solutions using either fixed or mobile integrated network databases, known as FIND and MIND. Both can be integrated into the existing computer-assisted verifications system in a country. In addition, MIND can be sued in a country without an existing system.

There are two main benefits of using FIND and MIND:

1. Access to international data
   —Data can be accessed real-time.
   —Quick searches: an automatic functionality sends queries to national and INTERPOL servers and provides responses from both simultaneously.
   —Top-level security systems to protect access to the data.
2. Integration into existing systems
   —No changes in the daily work of frontline officers and no special training required.
   —No language barriers, because the process is the same as when

officers conduct searches of their national databases.

—Easily adapted to individual countries' requirement and capabilities.

Which solution suits best?

This depends on the infrastructure in each country. MIND is proposed when a country cannot use FIND for whatever reason. INTERPOL officers will work with your country to identify the best technical platform for an integrated solution which satisfied your country's specific technical, legal and operational criteria.

How does it work?

An officer can submit a query to the national system by simply passing a passport over a digital scanner or manually entering its identification number. The response indicates whether or not the document matches one in the database.

The query passes simultaneously to a national database (if existing) and either the database at the INTERPOL General Secretariat (FIND) or a local copy of the data (MIND) via INTERPOL's I-24/7 global police communication network.

The officer will receive responses from both within seconds. And electronic alert system notifies member countries concerned of potential matches.

FIND—Fixed INTERPOL Network Database

This provides access to INTERPOL databases through online integration and allows communication between national computer servers and those at the INTERPOL General Secretaries (IPSG) via I-24/7.

1. The passenger produces the passport, which is scanned by the border control officer.

2. The passport is checked against the national database.

3. The passport is checked against the SLTD database at IPSG.

MIND—Mobile INTERPOL Network Database

This provides offline access to INTERPOL databases. Using I-24/7, ISPG can provide member countries with a copy of the data in its databases, which can be accessed locally through connection between existing national servers and the local copy of the data. MIND is controlled and updated by IPSG. Updates are automatic whenever new records are added.

1. The passenger produces the passport, which is scanned by the border control officer.

2. The passport is checked against the national database.

3. The national server checks the passport against the MIND device in the country.

4. The local MIND device contains a copy of the SLTD database at IPSG.

5. The SLTD system automatically updates records in the MIND device in the country.

What technical support is available?

Officers at the INTERPOL General Secretariat (ISPG) and in the National General Bureau (NCB) in your country will work to support you during installation and afterwards if required. The Helpdesk at IPSG is available around the clock to support the implementation of all steps.

Four steps to connection

1. Contact and introduction

—Initial contact between ISPG and the NCB in your country

—Contact person(s) from functional and technical sides established

—Presentation of functionalities and technical specifications of IPSG to users

—Principle agreement to go ahead with project

2. Assessment and action plan

—NCB writes a formal letter stating intention to set up an integrated system

—Joint team comprising members from IPSG, and NCB, country users and country technical specialists established

—Function and technical assessments carried out

—Action plan agreed, including timeline for implementation

3. Implementation and testing

—Implementation of technical specifications within the national infrastructure

—Functional and technical "live" tests between IPSG and specified police services in a country

—Confirmation that technical protocol works and application can be used in a country

4. Rollout and maintenance

—System made accessible to country's police services

—System assessed to ensure full working capacity and modified if required

—Ongoing support provided by IPSG Helpdesk as required

NOTE: Authorization to access INTERPOL's databases must be granted by NCBs in member countries. The NCB and all users must agree to the access rights and obligations prescribed by the organization.

(950 words)

Unit 9

Border Security and Management

Part Ⅰ In-class Reading

Pre-reading Questions

- *Why do you think border security and management is vital to the security of a country?*
- *After reading the following passage, could you find out the similarities and differences between the border management in the United States and in China?*

Text A

Border Security Oversight: Identifying and Responding to Current Threats

Thomas Homan

(Executive Associate Director of Enforcement and Removal Operations, ICE)

ICE primarily consists of two operational programs: Enforcement and Removal Operations (ERO) and Homeland Security Investigations (HSI).

ERO enforces the nation's immigration laws in a fair, prioritized, and effective manner. ERO identifies and apprehends criminal and other removable aliens, detains these individuals, and, guided by ICE's prioritized enforcement principles, removes individuals who are illegally present (or otherwise subject to removal) from the United States. HSI is responsible for a wide range of domestic and international criminal investigations arising from the illegal movement of people and goods into, within, and out of the United States, often in coordination with other federal agencies.

Over the past four years, ICE has focused its finite resources on the apprehension, detention, and removal of individuals who fall within our enforcement priorities. To this end, ICE has prioritized the removal of (1) aliens who pose a danger to national security or risk to public safety (including aliens engaged in or suspected of terrorism or espionage, criminal aliens, and aliens subject to outstanding criminal warrants, (2) recent illegal entrants, and (3) aliens who are fugitives or otherwise obstruct immigration controls. Through this focus, ICE has been able to help ensure public safety, and has seen unprecedented successes in enforcing the nation's immigration laws.

Overall, in fiscal year (FY) 2012, ICE's Office of Enforcement and Removal Operations (ERO) removed a record number of 409,849 individuals. Of these, approximately 55 percent, or 225,390, had a criminal conviction—almost double the total removals of criminals in FY 2008. This includes 1,215 aliens convicted of homicide, 5,557 aliens convicted of sexual offenses, and 40,448 aliens convicted for crimes involving drugs. Moreover, ICE also continues to make progress in the removal of other enforcement priorities. In FY 2012,96 percent of all ICE's removals fell into a priority category—a record achievement.

Prioritizing Recent Border Crossers

ICE's recent immigration enforcement successes are the result of smart, effective enforcement priorities. In order to help maintain control at our nation's borders, while at the same time managing limited resources, ICE prioritizes the identification and removal of recent border crossers and conducts targeted enforcement operations with U.S. Customs and Border Protection (CBP). This relationship with CBP is critical to DHS's enforcement success. More than half of the individuals removed by ICE in FY 2012 (240,363) were border removals (cases initiated by CBP, expedited removals, or removals of individuals within three years of entry into the United States). In addition, aliens referred to ICE by CBP currently represent 44 percent of all individuals in ICE detention on any given day.

Detention and Removal

- ICE Detention

Upon being taken into ICE custody, individuals are booked, fingerprinted, and photographed. Within 12 hours of arrival at a detention facility, each detainee receives an initial heath screening. This is followed by a comprehensive health assessment, including a physical examination and the completion of detailed medical history, within 14 days of their arrival.

ERO facilitates the processing of individuals in removal proceedings through the immigration court system and coordinates their departure from the country, including the preparation of necessary travel documents. Along the Southwest Border, Mexican nationals are largely removed via land transportation through U.S. Ports of Entry into Mexico. ICE removes Mexican nationals along the Southwest Border in accordance with agreements between the Government of Mexico, CBP and ICE.

Together with its DHS and Department of Justice partners, ICE carefully manages the detention population in its Southwest Border field offices to ensure that it can address the rapid and substantial changes in operational needs that can occur in the region. As this Subcommittee knows, border circumstances can quickly change. As a result, ICE has redoubled its efforts to be more nimble and smart as we respond to changing operational requirements, and we have the right polices and infrastructure in place to do just that.

• Removal Operations

In addition to removals to Mexico by ground transportation, removals may occur by commercial or charter flights. ICE Air Operations routinely depart from Mesa, Arizona; San Antonio, Texas; Alexandria, Louisiana; and Miami, Florida.

ICE Air Operations has provided transportation support to the Alien Transfer and Exit Program (ATEP). ATEP is a joint effort between ICE and CBP that allows for the transportation of aliens from an apprehending Southwest Border Patrol Sector for subsequent removal to Mexico through another Southwest Sector. The program is designed to deny, disrupt and dismantle the ability of alien smuggling organizations operating in the participating sectors. ATEP targets frequent recidivist illegal entrants, and other illegal aliens apprehended by CBP within the Laredo, Rio Grande Valley, and Tucson sectors.

ICE Air Operations is now preparing to commence Interior Repatriation Initiative (IRI) operations. On April 18, 2013, DHS signed an agreement with the Government of Mexico that created the framework for IRI. This initiative is designed to reduce recidivism and border violence by returning Mexican nationals to their cities of origin. In those locations, there will be a higher likelihood that they will reintegrate themselves back into their communities, rather than fall victim to human trafficking or other crimes in Mexican border towns. We expect to begin in summer 2013.

• Removal Proceedings and Criminal Prosecutions

ICE's Office of the Principal Legal Advisor (OPLA) has 26 Chief Counsel Offices around the country who litigate in removal proceedings before the Executive Office for Immigration Review. A total of 382,675 proceedings were completed in FY 2012. In addition, OPLA supports the U.S. Department of Justice's (DOJ) litigation of immigration appeals and federal litigation on behalf of ICE. OPLA's resources are focused on the agency's highest enforcement priorities, including criminal aliens and recent border entrants. In addition, OPLA has implemented a number of efficiencies in handling extensive caseloads in the immigration courts (such as developing pilot projects to establish formal expedited dockets in some localities, and working with DOJ to narrow contested issues in cases where courts are able to handle them on an expedited basis), while at the same time increasing the number of prosecutions for federal crimes.

OPLA also supports enforcement through targeted criminal prosecutions. In FY 2012, OPLA staffed 44 Special Assistant United States Attorney (SAUSA) positions nationwide. The SAUSAs assist U.S. Attorneys with increased caseloads that result from ICE's increased enforcement, and serve as critical force multipliers. ICE implemented the SAUSA initiative as a force multiplier in federal prosecutions focusing on immigration and customs-related criminal cases.

Detention Reforms

Also reflective of ICE's commitment to smart, effective immigration enforcement are the significant reforms we have made to the immigration detention system. Beginning in August 2009, these reforms address questions raised about ICE's immigration detention system, while allowing ICE to maintain adequate detention capacity to carry out our immigration enforcement responsibilities.

To help effectuate these reforms, in 2009 ICE established its Office of Detention Policy and Planning, which oversees day-to-day detention reforms while designing a new detention system consistent with our nation's values. ICE has also deployed nationwide a new automated Risk Classification Assessment instrument to improve transparency and uniformity in detention custody and classification decisions. This assessment instrument incorporates factors that reflect the agency's enforcement priorities and guides decision making regarding whether an individual should be detained or released on conditions, and if detained, the individual's appropriate custody classification level. The Risk Classification Assessment also provides an opportunity to identify victims of crimes, including human trafficking, and individuals who might face particular risks in detention due to age, health, disability, or sexual orientation or gender identity.

In addition, ICE has promulgated the 2011 Performance-Based National Detention Standards (PBNDS 2011), a revised set of national detention standards that better address the needs of ICE's detainee population. Among other things, these standards improve medical and mental health services maximize access to counsel and legal resources, reinforce protections against sexual abuse, augment religious opportunities, and enhance procedures for reviewing and responding to detainee grievances. Agreements to implement PBNDS 2011 are in place at ICE's largest detention facilities, accounting for approximately half of the agency's detainee population, and ICE is continuing to seek broader implementation of the standards through ongoing negotiations with detention facilities.

In addition, ICE has implemented strong safeguards against sexual assault in detention. These safeguards include a 2012 directive which establishes agency-wide policy and procedures with respect to prevention, response, and investigation of allegations of sexual abuse or assault for all detainees. The directive complements the mandates imposed on detention facilities by the new requirements of PBNDS 2011. This summer, DHS will also finalize new regulations, pursuant to the Prison Rape Elimination Act, which will build upon the zero-tolerance policy previously adopted for sexual abuse and assault at such facilities.

ICE continues to ensure the health and safety of detainees in our custody by enhancing oversight of detention facilities and improving conditions within the system. In addition, ICE's new detention standards place stricter limitations on the use of administrative segregation to protect vulnerable detainees and to house individuals with serious mental illness.

Other Key Border Security Efforts

- Border Enforcement Security Task Force

ICE has also improved border security by increasing our presence on the Southwest Border and strengthening our relationships with our law enforcement partners both domestically and internationally. ICE established the Border Enforcement Security Task Force (BEST) program, which leverages over 765 federal, state, local, and foreign law enforcement agents and officers representing over 100 agencies. Today, we have 35 BESTs: four along the Northern Border, 14 along the Southern Border, and 17 located at seaports across the country, including Puerto Rico.

BEST provides a co-located platform to conduct intelligence-driven investigations aimed at identifying, disrupting, and dismantling transnational criminal organizations that operate in air, land, and sea environments. In FY 2012, BESTs made 2,676 criminal arrests, 809 administrative arrests, and federal prosecutors obtained 1,419 indictments and 1,335 convictions in BEST investigated cases.

- Illicit Pathways Attack Strategy

Over the last few years, ICE developed the Illicit Pathways Attack Strategy (IPAS). IPAS supports the Administration's Strategy to Combat Transnational Organized Crime, an initiative launched in July 2011 that integrates federal resources to combat transnational organized crime and related threats to national security and public safety while urging foreign partners to do the same.

ERO contributes to IPAS by identifying known or suspected alien smugglers or persons being smuggled. These individuals, along with victims of human trafficking, are interviewed by ERO Intelligence Officers and information ascertained from these interviews is used in ERO lead intelligence reports. ERO lead reports are socialized with the intelligence community and the human smuggling and trafficking center for further analysis and utilization.

ICE's initial IPAS focused on high-risk human smuggling in the Western Hemisphere in order to identify and target human smuggling organizations and their pathways across the globe. ICE is currently expanding the IPAS model to include financial crime, in order to better combat transnational criminal organizations.

(1,546 words)

Background Information

▶ ICE

U.S. Immigration and Customs Enforcement is the principal investigative arm of the U.S. Department of Homeland Security (DHS). Created in 2003 through a merger of the investigative and interior enforcement elements of the U.S. Customs Service and the Immigration and Naturalization Service, ICE now has more than 20,000 employees in offices in all 50 states and 47 foreign countries. ICE's primary mission is to promote homeland security and public safety through the criminal and civil enforcement of federal laws governing border control, customs, trade and immigration. The agency has an annual budget of more than $5.7 billion, primarily devoted to its two principal operating components—Homeland Security Investigations (HSI) and Enforcement and Removal Operations (ERO).

▶ CBP

CBP is one of the world's largest law enforcement organizations and is charged with keeping terrorists and their weapons out of the U.S. while facilitating lawful international travel and trade. As the world's first full-service border entity, CBP takes a comprehensive approach to border management and control, combining customs, immigration, border security, and agricultural protection into one coordinated and supportive activity. The employees of CBP are responsible for enforcing hundreds of U.S. laws and regulations. On a typical day, CBP welcomes nearly 1 million visitors, screens more than 67,000 cargo containers, arrests more than 1,100 individuals and seizes nearly 6 tons of illicit drugs.

New Words

detain [dɪˈteɪn]

vt. 1) When people such as the police detain someone, they keep them in a place under their control. [正式]拘留

E.g. They are unarmed but have the right to detain any suspected wrong-doer until the police arrive.

2) To detain someone means to delay them, for example, by talking to them. [正式]耽搁

E.g. We won't detain you any further.

espionage [ˈɛspɪəˌnɑːʒ]

[U] *n.* Espionage is the activity of finding out the political, military, or industrial secrets of your enemies or rivals by using spies. 间谍活动

E.g. The investigation revealed they were involved in upwards of 100 projects of espionage or attempted espionage.

conviction [kənˈvɪkʃən]

[C] *n.* 1) A conviction is a strong belief or opinion. 坚定的信念

E.g. It is our firm conviction that a step forward has been taken.

2) If someone has a conviction, they have been found guilty of a crime in

a court of law. 判罪

E.g. He plans to appeal against his conviction.

[U] *n.* If you have conviction, you have great confidence in your beliefs or opinions. 坚信

E.g. He said he agreed but his voice lacked conviction.

nimble [ˈnɪmbəl]

adj. 1) Someone who is nimble is able to move their fingers, hands, or legs quickly and easily. 敏捷灵巧的

E.g. Heavier vehicles take longer to accelerate and stop, while smaller cars feel morenimble.

2) If you say that someone has a nimble mind, you mean they are clever and can think very quickly. 机智的

E.g. In the never-ending race to protect our country, we have to stay one step ahead of a nimble adversary.

recidivist [rɪˈsɪdɪvɪst]

[C] *n.* A recidivist is someone who has committed crimes in the past and has begun to commit crimes again, for example after a period in prison. 惯犯

E.g. Six prisoners are still at large along with four dangerous recidivists.

→派生词 recidivism [U] *n.*

E.g. Their basic criticism was that prisons do not reduce the crime rate, they cause recidivism.

caseload [ˈkeɪsləʊd]

[C] *n.* The caseload of someone such as a doctor, social worker, or lawyer is the number of cases that they have to deal with. (医生、社工或律师等需要处理的)案例数量

E.g. The caseload has increased 65% since 2008, when the federal government expanded law-enforcement efforts along the border.

custody [ˈkʌstədɪ]

[U]*n.* 1) Custody is the legal right to keep and take care of a child, especially the right given to a child's mother or father when they get divorced. 监护权

E.g. Gibson and Grigorieva are currently battling each other for custody of their 8-month-old daughter.

2) If someone is being held in a particular type of custody, they are being kept in a place that is similar to a prison. 拘留

E.g. The thief got nine months' youth custody.

promulgate [ˈprɒməlˌgeɪt]

vt. 1) If people promulgate a new law or a new idea, they make it widely known. 散布;传播

E.g. The company failed to promulgate new rules.

2) If a new law is promulgated by a government or national leader, it is publicly approved or made official. 颁布;公布

E.g. A new law was promulgated last month.

pursuant [pəˈsjuːənt]

adj. If someone does something pursuant to a law or regulation, they obey that law or regulation. 依照

E.g. If and when an investigation is appropriate in any matter, the Committee will carry out its responsibilities pursuant to our rules and with the utmost integrity and fairness.

leverage [ˈliːvərɪdʒ]

[U]*n.* Leverage is the ability to influence situations or people so that you can control what happens. 影响力

E.g. The more independent we are of Pakistan, the more leverage we have over Pakistan.

vt. To leverage a company or investment means to use borrowed money in order to buy it or pay for it. 举债经营

E.g. Leveraging the company is a big mistake.

Exercises

▶ Exercise One: Reading comprehension

Answer the following questions in your own words after reading the passage.

1. What is the function of Enforcement and Removal Operations (ERO)? And what is Homeland Security Investigations (HSI) responsible for?
2. What is the focus of ICE? With the focus, whom has ICE prioritized the removal of?
3. What are the ICE's recent enforcement priorities?
4. What is the Alien Transfer and Exit Program (ATEP)? And what is the purpose of designing ATEP?
5. What is the focus of ICE's Office of the Principal Legal Advisor (OPLA)?
6. Why did ICE establish the Border Enforcement Security Task Force (BEST) program? What can BEST provide?
7. Could you say something about the evolvement of the Illicit Pathways Attack Strategy (IPAS) developed by ICE?

▶ Exercise Two: Translation

Please translate the following sentences into Chinese.

1. ERO identifies and apprehends criminal and other removable aliens, detains these individuals, and, guided by ICE's prioritized enforcement principles, removes individuals who are illegally present (or otherwise subject to removal) from the United States.
2. HSI is responsible for a wide range of domestic and international criminal investigations arising from the illegal movement of people and goods into, within, and out of the United States, often in coordination with other federal agencies.

3. Together with its DHS and Department of Justice partners, ICE carefully manages the detention population in its Southwest Border field offices to ensure that it can address the rapid and substantial changes in operational needs that can occur in the region.
4. Beginning in August 2009, these reforms address questions raised about ICE's immigration detention system, while allowing ICE to maintain adequate detention capacity to carry out our immigration enforcement responsibilities.
5. This assessment instrument incorporates factors that reflect the agency's enforcement priorities and guides decision making regarding whether an individual should be detained or released on conditions, and if detained, the individual's appropriate custody classification level.

Part Ⅱ After-class Reading

Text B

Border Security: Examining B1/B2 Visas and Border Crossing Cards

Through specific intelligence and the use of sophisticated data systems, ICE identifies and tracks millions of foreign students, tourists, and temporary workers who are present in the United States at any given time. Visa overstays and other forms of nonimmigrant status violations bring together two critical areas of ICE's mission—national security and immigration enforcement.

Overstay Analysis Unit

The Department of Homeland Security (DHS) is focused on enhancing its vetting initiatives across the full mission space of homeland security by providing real-time biographic and biometric data to its front-line operational components while continuing to set leading biometric policies and standards. To this end, ICE's Overstay Analysis Unit (OAU) analyzes biographical entry and exit records stored in DHS's Arrival and Departure Information System (ADIS) to support the Department's ability to identify international travelers who have remained in the United States beyond their authorized periods of admission. DHS' Automated Biometric Identification System (IDENT) and ADIS provide person-centric information and enable DHS to search biometric and biographic data against government databases to establish and confirm the identities of individuals that DHS has already encountered. DHS's Office of Biometric Identity Management (OBIM) supports DHS components by returning any linked information from a match against its database to aid in their vetting of individuals already encountered by DHS to identify known or suspected terrorists, national security threats, criminals, and those who have previously violated U.S. immigration laws.

The OAU analyzes and validates two types of non-immigrant overstay records: out-of-country overstays (OCO) and in-country overstays (ICO). OCO records pertain to visitors who stayed beyond their authorized admission period and subsequently departed the country. The OAU validates these violations based on their reported departure dates and creates biometric and biographic lookouts for these subjects. The lookouts are posted in two separate databases: DHS' IDENT Secondary Inspection Tool and TECS, in order to alert and notify Department of State consular officers and CBP officers of a subject's violation before he or she is granted a visa or is readmitted to the United States. ICO records pertain to visitors with no evidence of departure or adjustment of status upon expiration of the terms of their admission.

The OAU makes overstay and status violation referrals from three unique sources, which apply to typical overstay violators, admitted watchlist subjects, and Visa Waiver Program (VWP) violators. The first source, non-immigrant overstay leads, is used to generate field investigations by identifying foreign visitors who violate the terms of their admission by remaining in the United States past the date of their required departure. The second source, admitted watchlist leads, monitors records for individuals who, at the time of admission to the United States, were the subject of a watchlist record containing derogatory information that did not render them inadmissible to the United States, but did warrant monitoring their visit. The third source is the Counterterrorism and Criminal Exploitation Unit's (CTCEU) Visa Waiver Enforcement Program (VWEP).

The Counterterrorism and Criminal Exploitation Unit

The CTCEU is the first national program dedicated to the enforcement of non-immigrant visa violators. Each year, the CTCEU analyzes records of hundreds of thousands of potential status violators after preliminary analysis of data from the Student and Exchange Visitor Information System (SEVIS) and the OAU along with other information. After this analysis, CTCEU determines potential violations that warrant field investigations and/or establishes compliance or departure dates from the United States. Between 15,000 and 20,000 SEVIS and ADIS records are analyzed each month and, since the creation of the CTCEU in 2003, over two million such records have been analyzed using automated and manual review techniques.

Today, through the CTCEU, ICE proactively develops cases for investigation in cooperation with the Student and Exchange Visitor Program and OAU. These programs enable ICE special agents to access information about the millions of students, tourists, temporary workers, and other nonimmigrants present in the United States at any given time, and to identify those who have overstayed or otherwise violated the terms and conditions of their admission. ICE special agents and analysts monitor the latest threat reports and proactively address emergent issues. This practice, which is designed to detect and identify individuals exhibiting specific risk factors based on intelligence reporting, including travel patterns and in-depth criminal research and analysis, has contributed to DHS's counterterrorism mission by initiating and supporting high-priority national security initiatives based on specific intelligence.

In order to ensure that the potential violators who pose the greatest threats to national security are given top priority, ICE uses intelligence-based criteria developed in close consultation with the intelligence and law enforcement communities. ICE chairs the Compliance Enforcement Advisory Panel (CEAP), comprised of subject matter experts from other law enforcement agencies and members of the Intelligence Community who assist the CTCEU in maintaining targeting methods in line with the most current threat information. The CEAP is convened on a tri-annual basis to discuss recent intelligence developments and update the CTCEU's targeting framework in order to ensure that the nonimmigrant overstays and status violators who pose the greatest threats to national security are targeted.

The third unique source for overstay and status violation referrals is CTCEU's VWEP. Visa-free travel to the United States builds upon our close bilateral relationships and fosters commercial and personal ties among tourist and business travelers in the United States and abroad. VWP, the primary source of nonimmigrant visitors from countries other than Canada and Mexico, currently allows eligible nationals of 37 countries to travel to the United States without a visa and, if admitted, to remain in the country for a maximum of 90 days for tourism or business purposes. Prior to the implementation of the VWEP in 2008, there was no national program dedicated to addressing overstays within this population. Today, ICE regularly scrutinizes a refined list of individuals who have been identified as potential overstays who entered the United States under the VWP. One of the primary goals of this program is to identify those subjects who attempt to circumvent the U.S. immigration system by obtaining travel documents from VWP countries.

In Fiscal Year 2012, the CTCEU received 38,335 B1/B2 violator leads. An automated vetting process closed 24,325 cases leaving 14,010 potential violators. The most common reasons for closure were subsequent departure from the United States or adjustment of immigration status to that of a lawful permanent resident. A total of 985 prioritized leads were sent to the field resulting in 253 arrests that met CTCEU's national security criteria. The remaining cases were referred to Enforcement and Removal Operations for possible enforcement action or closed.

ICE is proud of the good work accomplished over the last ten years to protect the integrity of our visa system. We are committed to promoting national security and have made significant progress in identifying visa overstay violators by working closely with our international, federal, state, local, and tribal partners to combat visa fraud and protect the integrity of our visa system.

(1,146 words)

Unit 10

Peacekeeping

Part Ⅰ In-class Reading

Pre-reading Questions

- *Please think about the existing significance of United Nations Peacekeeping. What does it bring to the peace of the whole world?*
- *Suppose you were a peacekeeping police officer, please figure out what you should pay attention to during carrying out a UN peacekeeping mission.*

Text A

The Basic Principles of United Nations Peacekeeping

Although the practice of United Nations peacekeeping has evolved significantly over the past six decades, three basic principles have traditionally served and continue to set United Nations peacekeeping operations apart as a tool for maintaining international peace and security:

* **Consent of the parties**
* **Impartiality**
* **Non-use of force except in self-defence and defence of the mandate**

These principles are inter-related and mutually reinforcing. Taken together, they provide a navigation aid, or compass, for practitioners both in the field and at United Nations Headquarters.

Consent of the parties. United Nations peacekeeping operations are deployed with the consent of the main parties to the conflict. This requires a commitment by the parties to a political process and their acceptance of a peacekeeping operation mandated to support that process. The consent of the main parties provides a United Nations peacekeeping operation with the necessary freedom of action, both political and physical, to carry out its mandated tasks. In the absence of such consent, a United Nations peacekeeping operation risks becoming a party to the conflict; and being drawn towards enforcement action, and away from its intrinsic role of keeping the peace.

This requires that all peacekeeping personnel have a thorough understanding of the history and prevailing customs and culture in the mission area, as well as the capacity to assess the evolving interests and motivation of the parties.

The absence of trust between the parties in a post-conflict environment can, at times, make consent uncertain and unreliable. Consent, particularly if given grudgingly under international pressure, may be withdrawn in a variety of ways when a party is not fully committed to the peace process. For instance, a party that has given its consent to the deployment of a United Nations peacekeeping operation may subsequently seek to restrict the operation's freedom of action, resulting in a *de facto* withdrawal of consent. The complete withdrawal of consent by one or more of the main parties challenges the rationale for the United Nations peacekeeping operation and will likely alter the core assumptions and parameters underpinning the international community's strategy to support the peace process.

The fact that the main parties have given their consent to the deployment of a United Nations peacekeeping operation does not necessarily imply or guarantee that there will also be consent at the local level, particularly if the main parties are internally divided or have weak command and control systems. Universality of consent becomes even less probable in volatile settings, characterized by the presence of armed groups not under the control of any of the parties, or by the presence of other spoilers. The peacekeeping operation should continuously analyze its operating environment to detect and forestall any wavering of consent. A peacekeeping operation must have the political and analytical skills, the operational resources, and the will to manage situations where there is an absence or breakdown of local consent. In some cases this may require, as a last resort, the use of force.

Impartiality. United Nations peacekeeping operations must implement their mandate without favour or prejudice to any party. Impartiality is crucial to maintaining the consent and cooperation of the main parties, but should not be confused with neutrality or inactivity. United Nations peacekeepers should be impartial in their dealings with the parties to the conflict, but not neutral in the execution of their mandate.

The need for even-handedness towards the parties should not become an excuse for inaction in the face of behavior that clearly works against the peace process. Just as a good referee is impartial, but will penalize infractions, so a peacekeeping operation should not condone actions by the parties that violate the undertakings of the peace process or the international norms and principles that a United Nations peacekeeping operation upholds. A mission should not shy away from a rigorous application of the principle of impartiality for fear of misinterpretation or retaliation, but before acting it is always prudent to ensure that the grounds for acting are well-established and can be clearly communicated to all. Failure to do so may undermine the peacekeeping operation's credibility and legitimacy, and may lead to a withdrawal of consent for its presence by one or more of the parties. Where the peacekeeping operation is required to counter such breaches, it must do so with transparency, openness and effective communication as to the rationale and appropriate nature of its response. This will help to minimize opportunities to manipulate the perceptions against the mission, and help to mitigate the potential backlash from the parties and their supporters. Even the best and fairest of referees should anticipate criticism from those affected negatively and should be in a position to explain their actions.

Non-use of force except in self-defense and defense of the mandate. The principle of non-use of force except in self-defense dates back to the first deployment of armed United Nations peacekeepers in 1956. The notion of self-defense has subsequently come to include resistance to attempts by forceful means to prevent the peacekeeping operation from discharging its duties under the mandate of the Security Council. United Nations peacekeeping operations are not an enforcement tool. However, it is widely understood that they may use force at the tactical level, with the authorization of the Security Council, if acting in self-defense and defense of the mandate.

The environments into which United Nations peacekeeping operations are deployed are often characterized by the presence of militias, criminal gangs, and other spoilers who may actively seek to undermine the peace process or pose a threat to the civilian population. In such situations, the Security Council has given United Nations peacekeeping operations "robust" mandates authorizing them to "use all necessary means" to deter forceful attempts to disrupt the political process, protect civilians under imminent threat of physical attack, and/or assist the national authorities in maintaining law and order. By proactively using force in defense of their mandates, these United Nations peacekeeping operations have succeeded in improving the security situation and creating an environment conducive to longer-term peace-building in the countries where they are deployed.

Although on the ground they may sometimes appear similar, robust peacekeeping should not be confused with peace enforcement. Robust peacekeeping involves the use of force at the tactical level with the authorization of the Security Council and consent of the host nation and/or the main parties to the conflict. By contrast, peace enforcement does not require the consent of the main parties and may involve the use of military force at the strategic or international level, which is normally prohibited for Member States, unless authorized by the Security Council.

A United Nations peacekeeping operation should only use force as a measure of last resort, when other methods of persuasion have been exhausted, and an operation must always exercise restraint when doing so. The ultimate aim of the use of force is to influence and deter spoilers working against the peace process or seeking to harm civilians; and not to seek their military defeat. The use of force by a United Nations peacekeeping operation should always be calibrated in a precise, proportional and appropriate manner, within the principle of the minimum force necessary to achieve the desired effect, while sustaining consent for the mission and its mandate. In its use of force, a United Nations peacekeeping operation should always be mindful of the need for an early de-escalation of violence and a return to non-violent means of persuasion.

The use of force by a United Nations peacekeeping operation always has political implications and can often give rise to unforeseen circumstances. Judgments concerning its use will need to be made at the appropriate level within a mission, based on a combination of factors including mission capability, public perceptions, humanitarian impact, force protection, safety and security of personnel, and, most importantly, the effect that such action will have on national and local consent for the mission.

The mission-wide ROE for the military and DUF for the police components of a United Nations peacekeeping operation will clarify the different levels of force that can be used in various circumstances, how each level of force should be used, and any authorizations that must be obtained by commanders. In the volatile and potentially dangerous environments into which contemporary peacekeeping operations are often deployed, these ROE and DUF should be sufficiently robust to ensure that a United Nations peacekeeping operation retains its credibility and freedom of action to implement its mandate. The mission leadership should ensure that these ROE and DUF are well understood by all relevant personnel in the mission and are being applied uniformly.

(1,421 words)

Background Information

▶ ROE (Rules of Engagement)

Rules of Engagement (ROE) are rules or directives to military forces (including individuals) that define the circumstances, conditions, degree, and manner in which force, or actions which might be construed as provocative, may be applied. They provide authorization for and/or limits on, among other things, the use of force and the employment of certain specific capabilities. In some nations, ROE have the status of guidance to military forces, while in other nations, ROE are lawful commands. Rules of Engagement do not normally dictate how a result is to be achieved but will indicate what measures may be unacceptable.

▶ DUF (Directive on the Use of Force)

Directive on the Use of Force (DUF) is the instruction to the police component on when and how force may legally be used by designated UN Police personnel to implement the mandate.

New Words

impartial [ɪmˈpɑːʃəl]

adj. Someone who is impartial is not directly involved in a particular situation, and is therefore able to give a fair opinion or decision about it. 公正的

E.g. The independent counsel act was designed to facilitate the appointment of impartial special prosecutors.

→派生词 impartiality [U] *n.* 公正

E.g. The investigation itself was given an added air of impartiality by the presence of 24 foreign experts from America, Australia, Britain and Sweden.

intrinsic [ɪnˈtrɪnsɪk]

adj. If something has intrinsic value or intrinsic interest, it is valuable or interesting because of its basic nature or character, and not because of its connection with other things. 内在的;本质的

E.g. And even when they disapprove of such activities they still seem to accept it as an intrinsic part of the game.

grudging [ˈɡrʌdʒɪŋ]

adj. A grudging feeling or action is felt or done very unwillingly. 勉强的

E.g. She grudgingly admitted that I was right.

rationale [ˌræʃəˈnɑːl, -ˈnæl]

[C] *n.* The rationale for a course of action, practice, or belief is the set of reasons on which it is based. 全部理由;根本原因

E.g. No matter what the reason or rationale, the move has got nations and corporations worried.

underpin [ˌʌndəˈpɪn]

vt. If one thing underpins another, it helps the other thing to continue or succeed by supporting and strengthening it. 支撑;加固

E.g. But what's revealing about this archive is how the personal stories underpin the politics.

→派生词 underpinning [C,U] *n.*

E.g. … the economic underpinning.

neutral [ˈnjuːtrəl]

adj. If a person or country adopts a neutral position or remains neutral, they do not support anyone in a disagreement, war, or contest. 中立的

E.g. Unlike some countries, neutral Burma did not offer bases from which to bomb its Indochinese neighbors.

[C] *n.* A neutral is someone who is neutral. 中立者

E.g. It was a good game to watch for the neutrals.

referee [ˌrɛfəˈriː]

[C] *n.* The referee is the official who controls a sports event such as a football game or a boxing match. 裁判员

E.g. The referee signals for extra time but Maradona decides the game will end there.

vt./vi. When someone referees a sports event or contest, they act as referee. 担任裁判

E.g. Vautrot has refereed in two World Cups.

penalize [ˈpiːnəˌlaɪz]

vt. If a person or group is penalized for something, they are made to suffer in some way because of it. 处罚

E.g. Some of the players may, on occasion, break the rules and be penalized.

rigorous [ˈrɪgərəs]

adj. 1) A test, system, or procedure that is rigorous is very thorough and strict. (测试、制度、程序)严格缜密的

E.g. They will be the most rigorous courses that are of real value to students.

2) If someone is rigorous in the way that they do something, they are very careful and thorough. 一丝不苟的;缜密的

E.g. He is rigorous in his control of his daily life.

retaliate [rɪˈtælɪˌeɪt]

vi. If you retaliate when someone harms or annoys you, you do something which harms or annoys them in return. 报复

E.g. India's actions were widely condemned by the international community and Pakistan was urged not to retaliate.

→派生词 retaliation [U] *n.* 报复

E.g. He said he needed the money to protect himself and his family against possible retaliation.

backlash [ˈbækˌlæʃ]

[C] *n.* A backlash against a tendency or recent development in society or politics is a sudden, strong reaction against it. (对政治或社会变化的)强烈反应

E.g. The clearest sign of dissatisfaction with the old order is the regionwide backlash against money politics.

deter [dɪˈtɜː]

vt. To deter someone from doing something means to make them not want to do it or continue doing it. 阻止

E.g. West Yorkshire Police are stepping up both visible and undercover patrols to deter anti-social behaviour.

calibrate [ˈkælɪˌbreɪt]

vt. If you calibrate an instrument or tool, you mark or adjust it so that you can use it to measure something accurately. 校准

E.g. No one can be certain which pricing schemes will best calibrate supply and demand.

de-escalate [diːˈɛskəˌleɪt]

vt. to reduce the level or intensity of (a crisis, etc.) 降低(危机等的)级别或强度

E.g. He urges respect for international humanitarian law and calls for de-escalation and calm to prevent any further bloodshed.

volatile [ˈvɒləˌtaɪl]

adj. 1) A situation that is volatile is likely to change suddenly and unexpectedly. 变化无常的

E.g. There had been riots before and the situation is volatile.

2) If someone is volatile, their mood often changes quickly. 情绪不稳定的

E.g. He is a volatile person who has no friend.

Exercises

▶ Exercise One: Reading comprehension

Answer the following questions in your own words after reading the passage.

1. What are three basic principles of United Nations peacekeeping operations?
2. What can the first basic principle (the consent of the main parties) provide for a United Nations peacekeeping operation?
3. What does the second basic principle (impartiality) mean?
4. What are the differences between robust peacekeeping and peace enforcement?
5. What instructions and directions can guide the use of force by a United Nations peacekeeping operation?

▶ Exercise Two: Translation

Please translation the following sentences into Chinese.

1. The fact that the main parties have given their consent to the deployment of a United Nations peacekeeping operation does not necessarily imply or guarantee that there will also be consent at the local level, particularly if the main parties are internally divided or have weak command and control systems.
2. A mission should not shy away from a rigorous application of the principle of

impartiality for fear of misinterpretation or retaliation, but before acting it is always prudent to ensure that the grounds for acting are well-established and can be clearly communicated to all. Failure to do so may undermine the peacekeeping operation's credibility and legitimacy, and may lead to a withdrawal of consent for its presence by one or more of the parties.

3. The environments into which United Nations peacekeeping operations are deployed are often characterized by the presence of militias, criminal gangs, and other spoilers who may actively seek to undermine the peace process or pose a threat to the civilian population.
4. In such situations, the Security Council has given United Nations peacekeeping operations "robust" mandates authorizing them to "use all necessary means" to deter forceful attempts to disrupt the political process, protect civilians under imminent threat of physical attack, and/or assist the national authorities in maintaining law and order.
5. The use of force by a United Nations peacekeeping operation should always be calibrated in a precise, proportional and appropriate manner, within the principle of the minimum force necessary to achieve the desired effect, while sustaining consent for the mission and its mandate.
6. In the volatile and potentially dangerous environments into which contemporary peacekeeping operations are often deployed, these ROE and DUF should be sufficiently robust to ensure that a United Nations peacekeeping operation retains its credibility and freedom of action to implement its mandate.

Part Ⅱ After-class Reading

Text B

China's Peacekeeping Organizations and Mechanisms

Leading Organizations, Functions and Decision-making

There are two organizations in China which are in charge of the domestic peacekeeping affairs. One is the Peacekeeping Affairs Office of the Ministry of National Defence of China, which was officially established in December 2001 and whose responsibility is to oversee the comprehensive management and coordination of the PLA's participation in the UN peacekeeping operations. The other is the Ministry of Public Security (MPS) who is in charge of peacekeeping affairs of police personnel under the direction of a leading group of MPS peacekeepers. Police peacekeepers are also usually selected from the Chinese People's Armed Police (PAP), a paramilitary police force tasked with internal security roles within China under the joint unified leadership of the Central Military Commission (CMC) and State Council. Although the Chinese military forces dominate the peacekeeping issue in China, police forces have become an important part of peacekeeping contributions and play a growing role in the new peacekeeping environment. The Ministry of Public Security has also established a peacekeeping office. Both military and police peacekeeping offices support each other and co-operate closely with other government organizations, like the Foreign Affairs Office of Minister of National Defence (MND), Ministry of Foreign Affairs and other organizations or branches.

The Peacekeeping Office of the MND is the main organization responsible for the organization, management and implementation of issues relevant to UN peacekeeping including the selection, training, deployment and rotation of personnel. It also has the responsibility of coordinating with other departments both inside and outside China. The Peacekeeping Affairs Office also designs, leads and monitors the military peacekeeping training program. At the beginning of 2002, China officially ascended to Level-Ⅰ of the UN Standby Arrangement System, confirming that its personnel had reached a high level of readiness to undertake peacekeeping operations. The Peacekeeping Affairs Office is also in charge of deploying peacekeeping contingents to mission areas within 90 days with 1x standard Engineering Battalion, 1x standard UN Level Ⅱ Hospital and 2x standard UN transport Companies.

When there is a requirement for a peacekeeping mission, after receiving the invitation by the UN and with the consent of concerned parties, the Peacekeeping Office of MND of China will coordinate with the relevant organizations like Ministry of Foreign Affairs and then report to the government for approval. Usually, the government will positively consider making its due contributions to the peace, stability and development of the regions in conflict.

Peacekeeping Training Programme

At the beginning of its participation, when it first decided to join the UNPKO, the Chinese military initially selected candidates from headquarters and military academies. Except for the physical fitness criteria, those who had relatively good knowledge of foreign languages, mainly from PLA International Relation College and University of Foreign Languages were more likely to be chosen. In the meanwhile, at the beginning in 1990s, China launched the first course to train military observers for UN peacekeeping at the PLA University of International Relations in Nanjing according to UN training standards, particularly with regard to training on policy, specialized skills and logistical support. According to an official from the Peacekeeping

Affairs Office, the selection of military observers and staff officers goes through a gradual process of recommendation at different levels, professional training for three to four months and they undertake an assessment examination. In order to meet the growing needs of peacekeeping training, in June 2009 the PLA officially opened its first and modern MND Peacekeeping Centre in Huairou District of Northern Beijing. This is believed to help centralize and better coordinate peacekeeping activities and provide a better platform for exchanging of peacekeeping experience. Therefore, China has progressively formed a relatively systematic mechanism for the selection and training of peacekeeping candidates.

In order to ensure the efficient performance of the peacekeeping mission and to illustrate the good image of the Chinese military, the Office of Peacekeeping Affairs often invites senior officers from headquarters, experts from the Ministry of Foreign Affairs, the Chinese Seismological Bureau and the General Administration of Customs to give lectures on the subjects such as international law, the UN Charter, the protection of human rights, providing humanitarian aid, the entry and exit of materials, disease prevention and control. In addition, drawing on the experience and good practice from foreign colleagues, China has invited more than 18 specialists from the British military to assist the pre-deployment training. After training, trainees are required to be familiar with and make good use of the UN working procedures, improve their English and strengthen their capabilities to carry out peacekeeping tasks. Then, those qualified officers are put into a reserve-candidate pool for timely deployment.

The Chinese police also have a similar procedure for the selection, training, deployment and management of both units and individuals being prepared for UN peacekeeping missions. Before first sending 15 civilian police to East Timor, the MPS trained the officers at PLA's College of International Relations in Nanjing in 1999. Then the MPS established its own peacekeeping course on the basis of the Chinese People's Armed Academy in August 2000, in Langfang City of Hebei Province. In 2004, China's Peacekeeping CIVPOL (Civilian Police) Training Centre was reconstructed at the expense of 160 million RMB and has become the largest peacekeeping civil police training centre in Asia. According to the 10th Anniversary Seminar of Peacekeeping Training hosted in November 2010, it has held 26 training courses for peacekeeping police officers, eight courses for riot police troops for 1,049 police personnel, three courses for liaison officers of 99 police officers and five courses of foreign police of 62 officers.

International Cooperation and other Activities

Based on these training centres, China's aim is to reinforce external exchanges and best practices with foreign counterparts as well as to promote friendly relations with foreign countries. China has facilitated extensive peacekeeping cooperation with the UN and other international organizations and regional institutions, through holding peacekeeping seminars. Consecutively for three years from 2004 to 2006, together with the British Military, China hosted three "UK-China Seminars on Peacekeeping Operations" in Beijing.

Furthermore, China has also enhanced the coordination and cooperation of peacekeeping at the international and regional level. In 2007 and 2009 respectively, the Peacekeeping Affairs Office of the MND hosted a China-ASEAN peacekeeping seminar reflecting China's determination to cooperate on peacekeeping, including training. In November 2009, China hosted the "Beijing International Symposium on UN Peacekeeping Operations", in which it participated with 6 international organizations including the UN and 22 individual nations. Most recently in September 2010, China hosted with the UN a senior commanders' peacekeeping training course in Beijing. All the trainees have the experience of participating in UN peacekeeping operations and have worked in command positions, with a good command of the

English language.

China also extended its peacekeeping efforts through active participation in bilateral and multilateral joint training exercises. In June 2009, The China-Mongolia "Peacekeeping" joint military drills were successfully conducted. In the words of the Deputy Chief of General Staff Ma Xiaotian, "It is not only the first training between China and Mongolia, but also the first joint training on the theme of peacekeeping held by the PLA with a foreign military." Such exchanges are not only essential to further contribute to world peace, but also helpful in strengthening mutual military trust between China and the rest of the world.

Principles of Participation in UNPKO

Based on the fundamental principles of UN peacekeeping, in order to safeguard justice and fairness of UNPKO and promote the efficiency of operations, China has also formed its own five special principles in line with the guidance of the purposes of the UN Charter. These are: Stress the importance of, and render support to peacekeeping activities in accordance with the tenets of the UN Charter; taking cognisance of the lead role of UN Security Council, peacekeeping operations should be carried out with the authorization and under the guidance of the Security Council; limited peacekeeping resources should be allocated to the most needed places and premature peacekeeping operations should not be undertaken when conditions are not yet ripe; double standards should be opposed during the planning and deployment of UNPKO; as an important measure for the UN to maintain peace and security, peacekeeping is not the only means, and priority should be given to the elimination of the root causes of conflicts, as well as comprehensive resolution through multi-tracked approaches.

Moreover, in terms of peacekeeping reforms in the UN, China advocates making better use of the holistic approach, adopting comprehensive management in peacekeeping operations, increasing the quality and integrity of peacekeepers to a higher standard, improving the efficiency and effectiveness of peacekeeping and promoting peacekeeping capacity building.

(1,430 words)

Case Analysis

Case One

Oregon Resident Convicted in Plot to Bomb Christmas Tree Lighting Ceremony

After a 14-day trial, Mohamed Osman Mohamud, 21, a naturalized U.S. citizen from Somalia and resident of Corvallis, Oregon, was convicted today by a federal jury in the District of Oregon of attempting to use a weapon of mass destruction (explosives) in connection with a plot to detonate a vehicle bomb at an annual Christmas tree lighting ceremony in Portland.

At sentencing, Mohamud faces a maximum statutory sentence of life in prison. Mohamud was arrested on November 26, 2010, after he attempted to detonate what he believed to be an explosives-laden van that was parked near the tree lighting ceremony in Portland. The arrest was the culmination of a long-term undercover operation, during which Mohamud was monitored closely for months as his bomb plot developed. The device was in fact inert, and the public was never in danger from the device.

"When an individual concocts a plan to commit mass violence—and is determined to follow through—law enforcement has an obligation to take action to protect the public. Today's verdict shows that they will be held to account," said Lisa Monaco, Assistant Attorney General for National Security.

"This trial provided a rare glimpse into the techniques al-Qaeda employs to radicalize home-grown extremists. With the verdict today, the jury has held this defendant accountable," said Amanda Marshall, U.S. Attorney for the District of Oregon. "I thank the dedicated professionals in the law enforcement and intelligence communities who were responsible for this successful outcome. I look forward to our continued work with Muslim Communities in Oregon who are committed to ensuring that all young people are safe from extremists who seek to radicalize others to engage in violence."

According to court documents and evidence presented by the government at trial, in February 2009, Mohamud began communicating via e-mail with Samir Khan, a now-deceased al-Qaeda terrorist who published *Jihad Recollections*, an online magazine that advocated violent jihad, and who also published *Inspire*, the official magazine of al-Qaeda in the Arabian Peninsula. Between February and August 2009, Mohamed exchanged approximately 150 e-mails with Khan. Mohamud wrote several articles for *Jihad Recollections* that were published under assumed names.

In August 2009, according to evidence presented at trial, Mohamud was in e-mail contact with Amro Al-Ali, a Saudi national who was in Yemen at the time and is today in custody in Saudi Arabia for terrorism offenses. Al-Ali sent Mohamud detailed e-mails designed to facilitate Mohamud's travel to Yemen to train for violent jihad. In December 2009, while Al-Ali was in the northwest frontier province of Pakistan, Mohamud and Al-Ali discussed the possibility of Mohamud traveling to Pakistan to join Al-Ali in terrorist activities. Mohamud responded to Al-Ali in an e-mail: "Yes, that would be wonderful, just tell me what I need to do." Al-Ali referred Mohamud to a second associate overseas and provided Mohamud with a name and e-mail address to facilitate the process.

In the following months, Mohamud made several unsuccessful attempts to contact Al-Ali's associate. Ultimately, an FBI undercover operative contacted Mohamud via e-mail under the guise of being an associate of Al-Ali's. Mohamud and the FBI undercover operative agreed to meet in Portland in July 2010. At the meeting, Mohamud told the FBI undercover operative he had written articles that were published in *Jihad Recollections*. Mohamud also said that he wanted to become "operational". Asked what he meant by "operational", Mohamud said he wanted to put an explosion together but needed help.

According to evidence presented at trial, at a meeting in August 2010, Mohamud told undercover FBI operatives he had been thinking of committing violent jihad since the age of 15. Mohamud then told the undercover FBI operatives that he had identified a potential target for a bomb: the annual Christmas tree lighting ceremony in Portland's Pioneer Courthouse Square on November 26, 2010. The undercover FBI operatives cautioned Mohamud several times about the seriousness of this plan, noting there would be many people at the event, including children, and emphasized that Mohamud could abandon his attack plans at any time with no shame. Mohamud indicated the deaths would be justified and that he would not mind carrying out a suicide attack on the crowd.

According to evidence presented at trial, in the ensuing months Mohamud continued to express his interest in carrying out the attack and worked on logistics. On November 4, 2010, Mohamud and the undercover FBI operatives traveled to a remote location in Lincoln County, Oregon, where they detonated a bomb concealed in a backpack as a trial run for the upcoming attack. During the drive back to Corvallis, Mohamud was asked if he was capable of looking at all the bodies of those who would be killed during the explosion. In response, Mohamud noted, "I want whoever is attending that event to be, to leave either dead or injured." Mohamud later recorded a video of himself, with the assistance of the undercover FBI operatives, in which he read a statement that offered his rationale for his bomb attack.

On November 18, 2010, undercover FBI operatives picked up Mohamud to travel to Portland to finalize the details of the attack. On November 26, 2010, just hours before the planned attack, Mohamud examined the 1,800 pound bomb in the van and remarked that it was "beautiful". Later that day, Mohamud was arrested after he attempted to remotely detonate the inert vehicle bomb parked near the Christmas tree lighting ceremony.

▶ Related Discussion about the case

1. Why does al-Qaeda begin to radicalize home-grown extremist? And what are the techniques al-Qaeda employs to do so?

2. Please discuss why Mohamud insisted to use the inert vehicle bomb and pick Christmas tree lighting ceremony as his target.

Case Two

Examples of Money Laundering Investigations

The following examples of money laundering investigations are written from public record documents on file in the court records in the judicial district in which the cases were prosecuted.

Dallas Lawyer Sentenced for Money Laundering

On September 26, 2013, in Dallas, Texas, Patrick Robert Simon was sentenced to 24 months in prison. Simon pleaded guilty in January 2013 to money laundering charges. According to court documents, during Fall 2009, Simon met with an individual to discuss putting aside proceeds from the individual's drug trafficking activities for his family's use while he was in prison for drug trafficking. After numerous meetings, on March 16, 2010, the individual met with Simon at Simon's law office to transfer the cash. Simon stated his scheme was that the individual was going to hire Simon's firm to handle the appeal of his drug trafficking conviction. Simon stated that he would then use his attorney trust fund to write a check every month to the individual's designcc. Simon explained that because it was a legal transaction, he would not have to report it. It was agreed that the checks would be written for $7,500, unless a different amount was specified later. The individual gave $110,000 in cash to Simon. Simon accepted the cash and during the time Simon was counting the cash, the three repeatedly discussed the individual's participation in the drug trade and that the money being counted was from his drug trafficking activities. Simon also instructed the individual on a code to use in all future communications to discuss the scheme.

Texas Man Sentenced for Role in "Black Market Peso Exchange" Scheme

On September 11, 2013, in Houston, Texas, Willie Whitehurst was sentenced to 151 months in prison for his role as one of the leaders of a criminal conspiracy that laundered more than $20 million through "shell" business bank accounts. In January and February 2013, Whitehurst and co-conspirators Enrique Morales, Fulton Smith and Anthony Foster pleaded guilty to conspiracy to commit money laundering and conspiracy to operate an unlicensed money transmitting business. Another co-conspirator, Sarah Combs, also pleaded guilty to conspiracy to operate an unlicensed money transmitting business. In August 2012, a federal grand jury in Houston indicted the five defendants for their parts in a large "Black Market Peso Exchange" scheme. From October 2009 to September 2011, the defendants placed United States currency gained through the sale of drugs into bank accounts held in the names of the organization's "shell" companies. The money was then transferred to different accounts in the United States and in Mexico. In exchange, pesos were transferred back to accounts owned by the organization's clients. Morales was previously sentenced to 188 months in prison, and Foster received a sentence of 121 months in prison. Smith was sentenced to 30 months, while Combs was sentenced to 24 months in prison.

Los Zetas Cartel Members Sentenced for Drug Trafficking and Money Laundering

On September 6, 2013, in Austin, Texas, Eusevio Maldonado Huitron, of Austin, was sentenced to 97 months in prison and three years of supervised release for his role in a complex conspiracy to launder millions of dollars in illicit Los Zetas drug trafficking proceeds. On May 9, 2013, a jury convicted Huitron of one count of conspiracy to commit money laundering. On September 5, 2013, Jose Trevino Morales, Francisco Colorado Cessa and

Fernando Solis Garcia were sentenced for their roles in laundering millions of dollars. Morales, of Balch Springs, Texas and Cessa, of Veracruz, Mexico, were each sentenced to 240 months in prison and three years of supervised release. Garcia, of Ruidoso, New Mexico, was sentenced to 160 months in prison and three years of supervised release. Morales and Cessa were convicted by a federal jury on May 9, 2013 of one count of conspiracy to commit money laundering. Evidence presented during trial revealed that Los Zetas is a powerful drug cartel based in Mexico and generate multi-million dollar revenues from drug trafficking. Since 2008, Miguel and Oscar Trevino Morales would direct portions of the bulk cash generated from the sale of illegal narcotics to Jose Trevino and his wife, Zulema Trevino, for purchasing, training, breeding and racing American quarter horses in the United States. Testimony also revealed a shell game by the defendants involving straw purchasers and transactions worth millions of dollars in New Mexico, Oklahoma, California and Texas to disguise the source drug money and make the proceeds from the sale of quarter horses or their race winnings appear legitimate. Furthermore, the defendants implemented a scheme to structure cash deposits in amounts under \$10,000 in order to circumvent mandatory bank reporting requirements. Over 400 quarter horses were seized by federal authorities and later auctioned for approximately \$9 million. The Government also seeks the forfeiture of real property; farm and ranch equipment; and funds contained in multiple bank accounts allegedly used in the defendants' scheme. The Government is also seeking a monetary judgment in the amount of \$60 million representing property involved in, and derived from, the conspiracy.

▶ Related Discussion about the case

1. Please discuss what money laundering means to transnational crimes.
2. What are the ways of money laundering mentioned in the cases?

Case Three

Gang-related Drug and Arms Trafficking Case

A federal grand jury in Sacramento has returned nine indictments charging 20 people with drug and arms trafficking by the Nuestra Familia prison gang and its affiliated Norteno gang members.

The indictments, returned on Thursday, are the product of a two-year collaborative investigation that focused on disrupting and dismantling a violent, gang-affiliated drug and weapons trafficking organization, according to Herbert M. Brown, special agent in charge of the Sacramento Division of the Federal Bureau of investigation.

The Nuestra Familia is described by authorities as a violent prison gang based in the California and federal prison systems, whose members exert control over street-level Norteno gang members engaged in drug trafficking and violent crime. During the course of the investigation, agents gathered evidence that many of the defendants were either members of the gangs or an associate of the Nuestra Familia, according to a federal Department of Justice news release.

Some of the defendants are alleged to have extensive criminal histories, including armed robbery, assault and drug distribution. According to information made public during bail hearings, large amounts of narcotics, firearms and cash were seized during the arrests in this operation last week.

According to court documents, Vidal Dominic Fabela, 45, Zebulen Cole Hughes, 20, Albert Miranda, 20, Angelo Lorenzo Gonzales, 27, Marion Hernandez Garcia, 35, Jaime Ysidro Sturgis, 37, Emilio Roberto Lopez, 19, Rudolph Edward Jimenez, 26, and Eleazar Guido Nunez, 21, all of

Sacramento, allegedly conspired to distribute and did distribute large amounts of methamphetamine in the Sacramento area. The indictment further charges Jose Andres Jaramillo, 35, a felon, with possessing a firearm that he distributed on behalf of Sturgis. In addition, Sturgis and Garcia were arrested on suspicion of possessing at least 50 grams of pure methamphetamine.

According to court documents, Alvaro Herrera, 29, Cilvino Dejesus Hernandez, 31, Arthur Albert Morales, 32, Juan Carlos Palacios Venegas, 42, and Rusty Allen Rycraft, 22, were charged with distribution of methamphetamine. Morales was also charged with possession of methamphetamine, and Rycraft was also charged with being a felon in possession of a firearm.

Also indicted were Jesse Anthony Montanez, 24, Sonny Melvin Gonzalez, 23, Ramon Jose Levario, 30, Zachary Kurtz, 21, and Robert Emilio Gonzalez, 31, all of Sacramento. All are accused of distributing methamphetamine in the Sacramento area. Levario, a felon, allegedly also sold a firearm to a confidential source. Some of these defendants have criminal histories that include assault, carjacking and drug distribution, authorities said.

▶ Related Discussion about the case

1. What is the relationship between the Nuestra Familia prison gang and the Norteno gang?

2. What are the features of the criminals discussed in the case?

Case Four

FBI Seeks Information Regarding Several Cyber Fugitives

The FBI announced today the addition of five individuals to its Cyber's Most Wanted and is seeking information from the public regarding their whereabouts. They are Farhan Arshad and Noor Aziz Uddin; Carlos Perez-Melara; Andrey Nabilevich Taame; and Alexsey Belan. Rewards ranging from up to $50,000 to $100,000 are being offered for information that leads to their arrest.

"The FBI will not stand by and watch our cyber adversaries attack our networks; we will track down and arrest individuals who have made it their mission to spy on and steal from our nation and citizens," said Richard McFeely, executive assistant director of the Criminal, Cyber, Response, and Services Branch. "Because cyber crime knows no boundaries, cyber criminals think they can hide overseas. But we are using our international partnerships and the publicity generated by our Cyber's Most Wanted to ferret them out."

Fugitives Farhan Arshad and Noor Aziz Uddin are wanted for their alleged involvement in an international telecommunications scheme and hacking venture to defraud individuals, telecom companies, and government entities in the United States and abroad, resulting in losses exceeding $50 million. It is alleged that between 2008 and 2012, Arshad and Uddin gained unauthorized access to business telephone systems and used those systems to initiate long-distance telephone calls to premium rate numbers through a scheme known as international revenue share fraud. The conspiracy caused the owners of the compromised telephone systems to be billed for services they neither ordered nor desired. Arshad and Uddin are part of an international criminal ring that the FBI believes extends into Pakistan, the Philippines, Saudi Arabia, Switzerland, Spain, Singapore, Italy, Malaysia, and other locations.

Arshad and Uddin were indicted for unauthorized access to a protected computer, conspiracy to gain unauthorized access to a protected computer, wire fraud, conspiracy to commit wire fraud, and identity theft.

Carlos Perez-Melara is wanted for his alleged involvement in manufacturing software that was used to intercept the private communications of hundreds, if not thousands, of victims around September 2003. As part of the scheme, Perez-Melara ran a website offering customers a way to "catch a cheating lover" by sending "spyware" disguised as an electronic greeting card. Victims who opened the card unwittingly installed a program that collected keystrokes and other incoming and outgoing electronic communications. The programs, created by Perez-Melara and known as "Lover Spy" and "e-mail PI," would periodically send e-mail messages to his customers, allowing them to obtain passwords, lists of visited websites, and intercepted e-mail messages of the intended victims.

Perez-Melara was indicted for manufacturing a surreptitious interception device, sending a surreptitious interception device, advertising a surreptitious interception device, advertising and promoting the surreptitious use of an interception device, intercepting electronic communications, disclosing electronic communications, and unauthorized access to a protected computer for financial gain.

The FBI is seeking Andrey Nabilevich Taame for his alleged involvement in Operation Ghost Click, a scheme that infected more than four million computers located in more than 100 countries from approximately 2007 to October 2011. At least 500,000 victims were in the United States. The scheme involved changing a computer's Domain Name System (DNS) settings. The DNS serves as a phone book for the Internet by translating domain names, such as www.fbi.gov, into Internet protocol (IP) addresses, thus allowing Internet traffic to be routed to the correct destination. As part of the scheme, Taame and six other individuals—who have since been arrested—used software that changed the victims' computers' DNS settings, therefore redirecting users' legitimate Internet traffic to websites users did not intend to visit. This allowed Taame and his co-conspirators to hijack Internet traffic to commit online advertising fraud by diverting traffic from websites with no commercial relationship to websites that pay for online hits.

Taame was indicted for wire fraud, unauthorized access to a protected computer, and conspiracy to commit both offenses.

Alexsey Alekseyevich Belan is wanted for his alleged involvement in the unauthorized taking of data from three U.S.-based companies in 2012 and 2013. It is believed Belan remotely accessed the victim companies' computer networks without authorization and thereby obtained information for the purposes of commercial advantage and private financial gain. Belan is also alleged to have knowingly possessed and used, without lawful authority, means of identification belonging to employees of the companies during and in relation to his unauthorized taking of the company data.

Belan was indicted for obtaining information from a protected computer, possession of 15 or more unauthorized access devices, and aggravated identity theft.

▶ Related Discussion about the case

Please discuss the methods adopted by these cyber fugitives.

Case Five

Mexican National Found Guilty on All Counts for Multiple Federal Sex Trafficking and Immigration Crimes

A federal jury returned guilty verdicts late today against AMADOR CORTES-MEZA, 36, of Tlaxcala, Mexico, on multiple charges of sex trafficking and human smuggling offenses related to a scheme to force young women and juveniles into prostitution. The jury found CORTES-MEZA guilty on all 19 counts after a trial lasting approximately two weeks.

United States Attorney Sally Quillian Yates said, "This defendant preyed on the most vulnerable of victims—girls and young women hoping for a better life—through promises of jobs or marriage. He then physically abused them, enslaved them, and forced them into prostitution. This trial provided a glimpse into the monstrous world of human trafficking."

According to United States Attorney Yates and the evidence presented in court: From Spring 2006 through June 2008, AMADOR CORTES-MEZA and others charged in the conspiracy recruited and enticed approximately ten victims to enter the United States illegally from Mexico and come to the Atlanta area. AMADOR CORTES-MEZA then forced them into prostitution for the financial benefit of the members of the conspiracy. He lured the young women and girls to the U.S. by promising better lives, legitimate employment, or romantic relationships with him. A brother and two nephews of AMADOR CORTES-MEZA were previously convicted after pleading guilty to sex trafficking charges related to this scheme.

Evidence at trial showed that after smuggling the victims into the United States, AMADOR CORTES-MEZA forced them to engage in prostitution by isolating them from their families, brutally beating them, and threatening to harm them and their loved ones. One victim testified that he told her that "he was going to hit her where it hurt the most" and she took that to mean he was going to go after her family. Another victim testified that the defendant told her he would kill her parents in Mexico if he was ever arrested. On a nightly basis, AMADOR CORTES-MEZA provided the victims to drivers who drove them to apartments and homes in Duluth, Chamblee, Canton, Marietta, Forrest Park, and as far away as Alabama and North Carolina to provide commercial sex to as many as 40 customers a night. The victims testified that the clients were charged $25-30 for ten to fifteen minutes of time with them, from which the drivers were given $10.

Witnesses at trial testified about brutal physical attacks from AMADOR CORTES-MEZA including one incident in which he beat a young woman with a rod and electric cord before throwing an iron at her head, slicing open her scalp. This woman testified that the defendant took the money she made because, in her words, she "was his property". Another witness testified AMADOR CORTES-MEZA beat her with a broomstick and a closet rod, ultimately breaking her finger. On the witness stand, she showed the jury her permanently disfigured finger. This same witness testified that after her first two days of forced prostitution she felt "destroyed". When she told the defendant she was in pain from the commercial sex acts he forced her to perform, AMADOR CORTES-MEZA replied that it "didn't mean a thing" to him and that she had to go to work the next day as well. Other victims recalled that on their first night of forced prostitution they had to perform sex acts with 20 to 27 total strangers.

Evidence at trial further showed that AMADOR CORTES-MEZA also prostituted girls he knew were under the age of 18. Two juveniles were smuggled into this country by AMADOR CORTES-MEZA, one of them when she was 14 years old. The defendant had been caught by authorities illegally crossing the border into Arizona with two of his victims, including one of the juveniles for whom he had obtained a fake birth certificate. After being deported, the defendant immediately re-entered the United States with both victims. AMADOR CORTES-MEZA told the fourteen-year-old he loved her, would marry her, and asked her to work in prostitution to earn money for their life back in Mexico. In reality, AMADOR CORTES-MEZA already had a wife and children in Mexico, but he kept that victim in prostitution for approximately three years. She testified about one incident during which AMADOR CORTES-MEZA pulled a knife on her and she thought that he was going to kill her.

Witnesses also testified that the defendant and his co-defendants strictly monitored the victims, keeping them under close supervision and control. The victims testified that they were terrified of AMADOR CORTES-MEZA and his associates, who required them to perform up to 40 acts of prostitution night.

The jury convicted AMADOR CORTES-MEZA on nineteen counts, after one day of deliberation. Those counts included offenses of sex trafficking by force, fraud, and coercion, sex trafficking of minors, conspiracy, importation and harboring of aliens for the purposes of prostitution, and smuggling aliens into the United States. AMADOR CORTES-MEZA faces a maximum sentence of life in prison. No sentencing date has yet been set by the Court.

The Department of Justice has identified human trafficking prosecutions such as this one as a top priority in the Department. In order to bring defendants to justice, victims of crime may be eligible for immigration status in the United States to assist in the prosecution. Nine of the victims addressed the court about what they suffered at the hands of this sex trafficking ring, telling of physical threats, beatings, and intimidation which caused them to work as prostitutes against their will.

▶ Related Discussion about the case

What features did the victims of human smuggling have in the case? How did the defendant and his co-defendants commit human smuggling?

Case Six

Two Iraqi Refugees in U.S. Charged in Terrorism-related Case

Two men are charged with sending cash, explosives and missiles to Iraq for use against Americans. Their case underscores gaps identified in the U.S. refugee vetting process before 2010.

Before he was granted refugee status in the U.S. and settled down in Bowling Green, Ky., Waad Ramadan Alwan was allegedly a sniper and skilled bomb maker who targeted U.S. forces and bragged that his "lunch and dinner would be an American".

Alwan is one of two Iraqi refugees who the Justice Department announced Tuesday had been charged with participating in an alleged plot to send cash, explosives and Stinger missiles to Iraq for use against Americans.

The men are among 56,000 Iraqis who took advantage of special programs to come to the United States after demonstrating they were in danger from Iraqi militias for their religious beliefs or because they were translators for U.S. government or media organizations.

Alwan was admitted into the U.S. in 2009 even though his fingerprint was found in 2005 on an unexploded roadside bomb that was set to blow up a U.S. convoy in Iraq, according to court documents. His print was loaded into a Defense Department database. But when he applied for U.S. refugee status, a search of that database was not yet a part of the application process.

Since then, those information-sharing weaknesses have been identified and corrected, said an official with the Department of Homeland Security.

Also, as new records go into the terrorist watch list, he said, refugees already in the U.S. are being vetted again.

When asked how men who actively fought against the U.S. in Iraq could have been allowed in the country, the official, who spoke on condition of anonymity because of the sensitivity of the information, said the case demonstrated that there were "specific gaps" in refugee vetting procedures before 2010.

Alwan, 30, and his cousin Mohanad Shareef Hammadi, 23, were arrested in Kentucky on May 25, and a federal grand jury returned the 23-count indictment the next day.

Charges against Alwan include conspiracy to kill U.S. nationals abroad, conspiracy to use a weapon of mass destruction against U.S. nationals abroad, attempting to provide material support to terrorists and to the insurgent group al-Qaeda in Iraq, and conspiracy to transfer, possess and export Stinger missiles.

Hammadi was charged with attempting to provide material support to terrorists and to al-Qaeda in Iraq and conspiracy to transfer, possess and export Stinger missiles.

Each faces life in prison if convicted.

Alwan had been under investigation since September 2009. According to charging documents that were unsealed Tuesday, Alwan recruited Hammadi to assist him, describing him as a relative who had worked as an insurgent in Iraq.

Over the course of a long undercover investigation, the documents say, Alwan and Hammadi picked up weapons provided by an FBI informant, at least some of them made inoperable by the FBI, and delivered them to a location believing they would be shipped to al-Qaeda in Iraq.

Starting in September 2010, the FBI informant told Alwan he was helping support insurgents in Iraq by smuggling weapons and money in used vehicles sent to Iraq. After that, Alwan and later Hammadi allegedly helped load into a tractor-trailer rocket-propelled grenade launchers, Kalashnikov PKM machine guns, sniper rifles, cases of inert C-4 explosives, two inert FIM-92A Stinger surface-to-air missiles and $100,000 cash, according to court documents.

There are no indications in the charging documents that Alwan or Hammadi had made plans to attack targets in the U.S.

In conversations with an FBI informant, Alwan described himself as a holy warrior, or "mujahid", who came to the U.S. because he was wanted in Iraq and a U.S. passport would allow him to travel freely, the documents say. "I didn't come here for America. I came here to get a passport and go back to Turkey, Saudi or wherever I want," Alwan allegedly said.

Experts said Alwan's and Hammadi's history of attacking U.S. troops should have been detected earlier. The FBI "may have done a good job preventing an incident. But it should have never gotten to that status. I still don't understand how he was able to get into the country," said Frank Cilluffo, who was White House domestic security advisor to President George W. Bush and is now the director of a domestic security studies program at George Washington University.

Iraqi refugees in the U.S. have come under renewed scrutiny in the last year and a half, ever since serious gaps were identified in the refugee vetting process. FBI Director Robert S. Mueller Ⅲ told a House hearing in February that he had information that al-Qaeda in Iraq may have used the weaknesses to send operatives to the U.S.

Related Discussion about the case

Please discuss the reasons why Alwan and Hammadi, Iraqi refugees, could get U.S. passport successfully, even they had the history of attacking U.S. troops before.

Case Seven

Illegal Gambling Networks Across Asia Targeted in INTERPOL-led Operation

An INTERPOL-coordinated operation targeting illegal soccer gambling networks across Asia during the 2014 FIFA World Cup has resulted in more than 1,400 arrests and the seizure of almost USD 12 million.

During the six-week operation, law enforcement officers from China, Hong Kong (China), Macao (China), Malaysia, Singapore and Vietnam carried out more than 1,000 raids on illegal gambling dens—many controlled by organized crime gangs—estimated to have handled around USD 2.2 billion worth of bets, the majority through illicit websites.

Operation SOGA V—short for soccer gambling—was the fifth action of its type since 2007 and was timed to target illegal soccer gambling activities from 1 June to 13 July, ahead of and during the 2014 FIFA World Cup.

Coordinated by INTERPOL's Criminal Organizations and Drugs unit and its Liaison Office in Bangkok, Operation SOGA V brought together officers from INTERPOL National Central Bureaus and other law enforcement agencies in the participating countries.

During the operation officers also seized computers and mobile phones which will be analysed to identify the potential involvement of other individuals or gangs across the region and beyond.

"The results of this latest Operation SOGA are significant in relation to the volume of bets being handled by these illegal gambling dens, as well as the number of arrests," said Jean-Michel Louboutin, INTERPOL's Executive Director of Police Services.

" Illegal gambling generates massive profits for organized crime networks which are often linked to corruption, human trafficking and money laundering, which is why a coordinated international response is required to tackle this type of crime.

"Operation SOGA V would not have been such a success without the hard work of the law enforcement authorities on the ground. INTERPOL will continue to support their efforts in identifying and dismantling the crime networks at the national, regional and global levels," concluded Mr Louboutin.

A meeting and training workshop involving participating countries and jurisdictions, in addition to representatives from the INTERPOL Asia Pacific Expert Group on organized crime, were held ahead of the operational phase.

The combined five SOGA operations have to date resulted in more than 8, 400 arrests, the seizure of almost USD 40 million in cash and the closure of some 3,400 illegal gambling dens which handled almost USD 5. 7 billion worth of bets.

With the organized crime networks behind illegal gambling dens often funneling their profits into other crimes including human and drugs trafficking, raising awareness of these hidden links is a key part of INTERPOL's Turn Back Crime campaign.

The campaign aims to highlight the dangers of organized and other forms of crime and to engage the private sector and the public, making them aware of the very real effects crime has on individuals' lives.

▶ Related Discussion about the case

1. What role did Interpol play when destroying illegal gambling networks?

2. Why is a coordinated international response required against illegal gambling?